Manager as Muse

*"It takes two men to produce a work of art,
one to paint it and the other to hit him over the head
just before he spoils it."*

- Martin Lewis, artist, quoted in Robert Raynolds,
Thomas Wolfe: Memoir of a Friendship; Austin and London:
University of Texas Press, 1964

Manager as Muse

Maxwell Perkins' Work with
F. Scott Fitzgerald,
Ernest Hemingway,
and Thomas Wolfe

Kathleen Dixon Donnelly, Ph.D.

Copyright © 2014 Kathleen Dixon Donnelly

All Rights Reserved

This publication may not be reproduced, stored in a retrieval system, or transmitted in whole or in part, in any form or by any means, electronic, mechanical, photocopying, recording, or otherwise—with the exception of a reviewer who may quote brief passages in a review to be printed in a newspaper or magazine—without prior written permission from the author. Contact the author: **kaydee@gypsyteacher.com**.

ISBN-13: 978-1-503112315

ISBN-10: 1503112314

Book design by Jean Boles
http://jeanboles.elance.com

Dedication

To my "unshaken friends."

Acknowledgements

In my original 1983 thesis for my MBA at Duquesne University in Pittsburgh, PA, I thanked the following people:

Dr. John South, Dr. Bernadine Meyer, and Mr. R. Stanley Seymour for their help in the preparation and organization of the original proposal and for their suggestions throughout the work;

Dr. South especially for his encouragement over the extended period this work required; and

Mr. Charles Scribner, Jr., for his graciousness in allowing me to interview him for a 'business' thesis which he considered irrelevant to his friend, Maxwell Perkins.

Acknowledgement must also be made of the patience of all those concerned, including the Pennsylvania Higher Education Assistance Association [PHEAA], my father and friends who listened to the ideas as they formed, and especially those to whom this work is dedicated.

The version presented here has been cut down to focus, not on the academic theory required in a thesis, but on the relationships between Maxwell Perkins and his writers, and what managers of creative people today can learn from them. Despite the dramatic changes in the publishing industry in the past thirty years, I have not felt the need to substantially update the text. The principles remain the same.

I would also like acknowledge A. Scott Berg's excellent biography *Max Perkins: Editor of Genius,* soon to be a major motion picture starring Colin Firth and Jude Law, upon which I depended greatly.

For this version I would also like to add thanks to David Hope, who first alerted me to the resurgence in interest in Perkins;

Anton Perreau, who got me started;

Howard Manns who led me to Jean Boles, an excellent guide through the process;

Nicola Jones and Fiona Joseph, whose brainstorming came up with some great ideas;

Tony, Willie and Gussie, who encouraged and supported me; and all my other 'unshaken friends' who have listened to endless tales about the 1920s over the past years.

For other essays, articles, and information about presentations concerning these creative people and others, see www.suchfriends.wordpress.com, or follow me @SuchFriends.

For more information, you can contact me directly at kaydee@gypsyteacher.com.

Contents

I Introduction 13
II Henri Fayol 19
Henri Fayol (1841-1925) 19
Fayol's Principles 21
    1) Equity 23
    2) Discipline 24
    3) Remuneration of Personnel 24
    4) Unity of Command 25
    5) Subordination of the Individual to the General Interest 26
Significance and Criticism of Fayol's Work 27
III Maxwell Perkins 29
The Role of the Editor in Perkins' Time 29
Scribner's 34
Maxwell Perkins (1884-1947) 38
    Relationship with Scribner's 47
    Relationships with Authors 51
    Influence 57
Photo Gallery of Other Perkins' Authors 58
IV Maxwell Perkins and F. Scott Fitzgerald, Ernest Hemingway and Thomas Wolfe 63
F. Scott Fitzgerald 65
    Work Habits 68
    Relationship with Perkins 72
    Money 73
    Friendship 81

Short Story Collections and Other Works	84
Involvement in Their Personal Lives	87
This Side of Paradise and *The Beautiful and Damned*	89
The Great Gatsby	93
Tender Is the Night and *The Last Tycoon*	100
Ernest Hemingway	106
Work Habits	111
Relationship with Perkins	115
Non-Fiction Works and Short Stories	121
The Sun Also Rises	129
A Farewell to Arms	133
For Whom the Bell Tolls	136
Thomas Wolfe	139
Work Habits	143
Relationship with Perkins	147
Look Homeward, Angel	161
Of Time and the River	167
The Break between Perkins and Wolfe	184
Posthumous Works	201
V Conclusions	207
Application of Principles	207
Equity	207
Discipline	208
Remuneration of Personnel	208
Unity of Command	210
Subordination of the Individual to the General Interest	211
Applications to Specific Authors	212

The "Perkins Principles" 214
    A Matter of Priorities 214
    The Power of Suggestion 215
    Room for Growth 216
Conclusion 217
Bibliography 219
About the Author 229

I

Introduction

When I first met with Charles Scribner, Jr., president of Charles Scribner's Sons, in May of 1980, to discuss Maxwell Perkins and his influence on writers and publishing, Mr. Scribner expressed his doubt about the relevance of Perkins to research for an MBA thesis. "When I read your letter, Miss Donnelly," he said, "I was quite surprised. My goodness, Maxwell Perkins was one of the worst businessmen who ever lived."

This statement has been applied to many managers and supervisors who work so well with their creative employees that they are considered to be bad businessmen. These managers encourage creative ideas, earn respect and often, but not always, friendship, and push the creative workers to achieve more than they could have on their own.

But these characteristics do not necessarily make a bad businessman. Many of Perkins' decisions were not good for his company, Scribner's, in the short run. But in the long run many of those decisions served the company—and his authors—well.

Creative people have often been viewed as aberrations in the business setting, a little bit different, a little eccentric, and sometimes a lot of trouble. Since I researched this topic in the early 1980s, there has been a greater realization of the importance of creative thinking and innovation to all organizations, not only high tech start-ups in California.

This has put the spotlight on the importance of those tasked with managing creative people within all types of businesses. Publishers, like many other organizations, must work with many creative people, primarily writers, and the person within the publishing organization who must devote his or her attention to working with the writer to produce a work of literature is still the editor.

Traditionally editors are anonymous personages who work behind the scenes. Although it is hard to pinpoint an editor's exact influence on a writer's work, the editor's role is crucial to the financial and literary success of a book. We don't always know what great writers, still unknown and unpublished, were passed over by editors lacking insight, but we do know of some truly creative editors who shaped authors and their works into successful novels and works of non-fiction.

Maxwell Perkins, although not as famous as his best-known authors—F. Scott Fitzgerald, Ernest Hemingway and Thomas Wolfe—became legendary in publishing for his talent in working with writers. Early in his career, particularly through his work with Fitzgerald, Perkins was known as an editor who truly helped authors, and this led many of the young writers of his day to seek him out. Ring Lardner (*You Know Me, Al*), Marjorie Kinnan Rawlings (*The Yearling*), Marcia Davenport (*East Side, West Side*), Erskine Caldwell (*Tobacco Road*), and James Jones (*From Here to Eternity*) were among his "lesser" finds.

Perkins did much more than edit copy. He motivated his authors when they needed it, restrained them when he saw they were wasting themselves, supported them emotionally as a friend, father or doting uncle, and financially to see them through frantic periods of work and long dry spells lacking in inspiration. He stood up to the Scribner's management for the authors' works when he believed it was for the good of his writers as well as the company. In the words of his biographer, A. Scott Berg (1978), "Beginning with Fitzgerald..., Perkins slowly altered the traditional notion of the editor's role."

Although Perkins, his authors and their relationships are unique, their combined efforts were so successful, and Perkins' own managerial techniques were so insightful and effective, they are worthy of exploration from the point of view of management.

When I embarked on the research for this thesis as part of my MBA at Duquesne University in Pittsburgh, PA, my objectives were to focus on the relationships Perkins established with each of his three major authors, analyze their work together to determine how he motivated them, and suggest ways in which managers in other situations could apply these same techniques to their own creative employees. My focus was on Perkins' behavior, not that of his writers. By studying a manager who is considered to be one of the best in his field, it was hoped that general principles could be extracted which other managers could use in working with creative people in all fields.

To do this, I used as a framework the principles of Henri Fayol. Management theory was probably unknown to Perkins, although he and Fayol were roughly contemporaneous. However, Fayol's concept of determining general guidelines from actual experience fit conceptually with the purpose of my thesis.

Like Fayol, I assumed that looking at a successful manager's experience could lead to some general principles for others. His goal was to set down in writing what he had learned from his own experience, making it clear that his guidelines were neither definitive nor complete.

My research was not based on the assumption that the way Perkins worked is precisely the way all managers in all fields should work. My assumption was that Perkins did use certain techniques in working with three unusually creative writers and that his success can serve as a guide to others. Except for my interview with Mr. Scribner, who knew Perkins personally and passed on many first hand insights on his impact on the writers as well as the company, I used secondary sources, primarily biographies, published collections of letters and other studies of their work. I have referenced all these throughout this book, but any information collected during the interview, I refer to as being from 'Mr. Scribner.'

My most important secondary source was the excellent biography, *Max Perkins: Editor of Genius*, by A. Scott Berg (1978). In addition, I found, in those pre-internet, pre-Google days of research, an invaluable unpublished dissertation, *Thomas Wolfe and His Scribner's Editors*, by Francis Skipp (1962).

The only absence of letters to and from Perkins is in the case of Hemingway, who decreed in his will that his letters never be published. Biographers and critics circumvented this rule by paraphrasing his salty and colorful language, and quoting short excerpts with the permission of his widow, Mary. Unfortunately, this made direct quotes awkward at best. Carlos Baker, Hemingway's official biographer, with Mary's consent, published *Selected Letters, 1917-1961* (1981) during the writing of my thesis. It was too late in my research process to go back and find direct quotes, so I have left the paraphrasing as it was.

To come up with guidelines for other managers of creative people, I used content analysis of all the material gathered. The details of this analysis have been left out of this version, to keep the focus on the relationships between Perkins and these three writers. They are contained in the full thesis available at www.lulu.com/spotlight/suchfriends.

Perkins has been studied before; his writers have been studied at great length; managers and creative people have been researched, interviewed, measured and evaluated before. However, Perkins' work has not been studied with reference to general principles of management. Hopefully, 30 years on, my research will prove to still be of interest to managers as well as those who are fans of American literature.

II

Henri Fayol

Henri Fayol (1841-1925)

Henry Fayol

Maxwell Perkins was probably not aware of any management theories, although they were developing as he succeeded in a job which included supervising extremely creative and independent people. However, for the purposes of my MBA thesis, I chose to use the work of one of the earliest theorists, French businessman Henri Fayol, because his approach of developing principles out of personal experience fit my case study best.

Fayol spent a large part of his career as an executive, and also an engineer, taking orders as well as giving them. He worked from 1860 to his retirement in 1918 for the same company, Commentry-Fourchambault, known as Comambault, and was a director of the firm until his death in December 1925. When he published his only major work, *General and Industrial Administration* (1916), he had spent 28 years as managing director of the coal mining company, taking it from near bankruptcy to major contributions to the French war effort. Passing one's career entirely with one organization was more common in that time than now, especially in Europe, and Perkins' career took the same path.

Fayol's book simply proposed the principles he had found useful in turning around the hopeless situation his company was in when he took over. His training as an engineer did not necessarily prepare him for management, and this lead him to become one of the first theorists to formulate the administrative function of management as distinct from the technical function.

After retiring from his job, Fayol devoted himself to popularizing his theory, writing pamphlets applying the principles to military administration, and trying to convince the government to pay attention to his principles. Fayol's ideas caught on immediately in France. However, his retiring personality hindered the spread of his work. Although he loved discussing his ideas with others, Fayol had little taste for publicity. Four years after his death his book of fewer than 100 pages was translated into English. But it was another 20 years before his work became known in the United States. One of the reasons was the translation of the title as *General and Industrial Administration*, leading Americans to believe that the book dealt with public administration. In 1949 Pitman in London published a new translation under the title of *General and Industrial Management* and Fayol's work became more generally known (*Business Week*, 1978). All references in this book are to this 1949 edition.

Contrary to other theories of the time, Fayol believed in the value of the individual: "Each employee, intentionally or unintentionally, puts something of himself into the transmission and execution of orders; he does not operate merely as a cog in the machine." He was a participant observer, and his assumption was that the techniques of the successful manager—namely himself—could be described and taught. He found the elements of administration to be planning, organizing, coordinating, and controlling, familiar words to students in today's management classes.

Fayol saw organization as a process, not a given. He placed great emphasis on daily to ten-yearly forecasts, weekly meetings and organization charts because of the ease with which they can be reviewed (Chambers, 1974).

All of Fayol's contributions were from the point of view of the general manager and revolve around two central ideas, (1) the distinction between the administrative function of a business and other activity, and (2) the emphasis which executives and supervisors give to this in relation to their other duties (Pearson, 1945). The major task of the head of any organization, in Fayol's view, was *prevoyance*, or forecasting and planning. He felt that all employees needed some managerial ability, but they needed progressively more at higher levels of the organization.

Fayol's Principles

Central to Fayol's theory is the concept of principles of management, which he summed up best:

> To me it seems at the moment especially useful to endow management theory with a dozen or so well-established principles...I have simply expressed my personal opinion in connection with them. Are they to have a place in the management code which is to be built up? General discussion will show.

His principles were flexible and adaptable: "Seldom do we have to apply the same principle twice in identical conditions; allowance must be made for different changing circumstances."

This is how Fayol listed his 14 principles:

1) Division of work
2) Authority
3) Discipline
4) Unity of command
5) Unity of direction
6) Subordination of individual to the general interest
7) Remuneration of personnel
8) Centralization
9) Scalar chain (line of authority)
10) Order
11) Equity
12) Stability of tenure of personnel
13) Initiative
14) *Esprit de corps*

Although Fayol resisted attempts to classify and reorganize these, other analysts have succumb. Gibson, et al (1976) provide the simplest classification, grouping them as Structure, Process and End-result principles. Here is their categorization:

Structural

- Division of work
- Unity of direction
- Centralization
- Authority/Responsibility
- Scalar chain

Process

- Equity
- Discipline
- Remuneration of personnel
- Unity of command
- Subordination to general interest

End-Result

- Order
- Stability
- Initiative
- *Esprit de corps*

My emphasis was on Process principle because these deal most specifically with the editor-author relationship.

1) Equity

"Desire for equity and equality of treatment are aspirations to be taken into account in dealing with employees...The head of the business must frequently summon up his highest faculties. He should strive to instill a sense of equity throughout all levels of the scalar chain." —Henri Fayol

This principle involves protecting employees from unfair practices of owners, as well as protecting owners from excessive wage demands. Equity underlines *esprit de corps* and connotes sensitivity to the spirit of regulations, a "mixture of inspired common sense and human wisdom" (Gibson, et al, 1976).

2) Discipline

"Discipline is in essence obedience, application, energy, behavior, and the outward marks of respect observed in accordance with the standing agreement between the firm and its employees...When a defect in discipline is apparent or when relations between superiors or subordinates leave much to be desired, responsibility for this must not be cast...on the poor state of the team, because the ill mostly results from the ineptitude of the leaders. Experience and tact on the part of a manager are put to the proof in the choice and degree of sanctions to be used...Individual people and attendant circumstance must be taken into account."   —Henri Fayol

Fayol believed this principle to be essential to an organization's success and to be based on respect rather than fear. "Poor discipline was inevitably the result of poor leadership and good discipline came from good leaders," said Wren (1972).

3) Remuneration of Personnel

"Remuneration of personnel is the price of services rendered. It should be fair and...afford satisfaction both to personnel and firm...The rate of remuneration depends, firstly, on circumstances independent of the employer's will and employee's worth, viz. the cost of living, abundance or shortage of personnel, general business conditions, the economic position of the business, and after that it depends on the value of the employee and mode of payment adopted."   —Henri Fayol

Fayol identified three types of payment—time rates, piece rates, and job rates, or "Payment made turning upon the execution of a definite job set in advance and… independent of the length of the job." This is the method of payment used for authors in Perkins' time. But Fayol also cautioned that neither the method nor the rate of payment "absolves management from competence and tact, and keenness of workers and peaceful atmosphere of the workshop depend largely upon it." Fair remuneration must reflect the fair rate of exchange for services, and also reflect the equity principle.

Fayol rather naively believed that "managers have no need of monetary incentive to carry out their duties, but they are not indifferent to material satisfaction…The hope of extra profit is capable of arousing their enthusiasm." He also encouraged managers to take a keen interest in the "health, strength, education, morale, and stability of [their personnel]," although he acknowledged that this raises a question of how much interest an employer should have in the lives of his workers outside the workplace. This became an issue with Perkins' relationship with his writers, particularly Wolfe.

4) Unity of Command

"For any action whatsoever, an employee should receive orders from one superior only…Should this be violated, authority is undermined, discipline is in jeopardy, order disturbed, and stability threatened." —Henri Fayol

Any subordinate having one superior minimizes ambiguity and actually relates more to the behavior of managers than the design of the organization. Fayol's caution is to managers not to bypass a superior when dealing with a subordinate.

Although Fayol believed that the scalar chain and unity of command were important relative to communication within an organization, he recognized that "they can be slow and in big enterprises take disastrously long. Respect for the hierarchic channels must be reconciled with the need for quick action." Fayol also advised against "abuse of written communication," encouraging managers to give orders verbally because "it is well known that differences and misunderstandings which a conversation could clear up, grow more bitter in writing" (Dyer and Dyer, 1969). Anyone who has had an e-mail misinterpreted would certainly agree.

5) Subordination of the Individual to the General Interest

> "The interest of one employee or group of employees should not prevail over that of the concern; ...the interest of the home should come before that of its members, and... the interest of the state should have pride of place over that of one citizen or group of citizens." —Henri Fayol

This rule gives managers a way to resolve conflicts. It reflects the importance of every member in the organization knowing the goals as well as feeling and absorbing them. Mooney (1947) uses this telling example from the arts:

> In the coordination of [an orchestra] the purpose is the production of a collective harmony, not as a means to an end but as an end in itself. To attain this end each individual musician merges himself in the common purpose...In the orchestra, these individual functions derive their importance solely from their contributions to the common purpose, and the relation of each musician's function to this purpose is ever present in the instant result. The orchestra [is] the supreme symbol and the simplest illustration of a coordinated effort.

Significance and Criticism of Fayol's Work

What place does Fayol's theory occupy today? His isolation of the elements of his own success was a unique contribution to the infant study of management. "For the first time a successful business leader of long experience submitted, not the work of others, but his own duties and responsibilities to close scientific analysis. He viewed what he had to do as an administrator with a detachment as rare as it is valuable," according to Urwick (1969).

He was also the first to support training managers how to manage, starting early and at the bottom. As Pearson (1945) says,

> Frequently a top notch engineer who has become head of his technical department fails as a general manager. But to what extent is it recognized that when an engineer succeeds as general manager of a large enterprise it may be due more to success in coping with "administration" than to his knowledge of engineering? Fayol deduced this truth many years ago and constantly stressed the need for including training for the "administrative function" in the engineering curriculum.

His influence today, like that of most classic management theorists, has waned quite a bit, although at one time he was known as "Europe's most influential management practitioner and philosopher" (*Business Week*, 1978). Others have criticized his principles as too broad to be of much help, and some say they have no universality of application.

Although Fayol's principles and Perkins' work are now long in the past, my research was based on the assumption that those managing creative people today can still learn from these men's experiences.

III

Maxwell Perkins

The Role of the Editor in Perkins' Time

In the thirty-plus years since I researched the field, publishing has undergone radical changes. No more need for would-be authors to wait around for agents and editors to find them. Everyone with access to the internet and MS Word can be a publisher now. Because the technology and the dynamics of the business have changed drastically, it is worth it to go back and look at what American publishing was like in Perkins' day.

Before 1830 books published in America were 70% British, and no author, including the stars such as Washington Irving, lived by writing alone. (He had great inheritances.) Publishers also had other sources of income, usually bookstores or printing plants (Tassin, 1914a).

As publishing became more American, authors became more aggressive. They asked for money and got it; they began the long tradition of gossip among the New York literati; and they sold their copyrights for large fees, although there was not yet any international copyright to protect them (Tassin, 1914b).

In the second half of the 19th century, publishers began the practice of initiating ideas and finding authors to write them. Royalties still varied, but 10% began to be accepted as standard. A new tradition appeared—the literary agent (Tassin, 1914c; Burlingame, 1946).

Near the turn of the century, newspaper printing shops became unionized. Young boys could no longer sign up to run errands at the local paper, as Mark Twain had, as a first step to becoming a writer. Instead, Theodore Dreiser, HL Mencken, Stephen Crane and others had to serve their apprenticeships as cub reporters on daily newspapers in large cities. After World War I, this was no longer possible because of the fierce competition for such jobs. After a while, young Hemingways did not go off to the Kansas City Star to become famous writers, but to become journalists, a profession in its own right (Cowley, 1950).

The new century started out well for the book publishing business. 8,000 titles were produced in 1901 and by the end of the decade that number had increased to 13,000, but only about 2% of the manuscripts submitted to publishers (Brett, 1913).

After the war, publishing houses began to branch out into magazines, medical and legal books, and textbooks. Distribution was one of publishing's biggest problems, as they were totally dependent on booksellers to get their product to market. The average book cost less than 50 cents for manufacturing and the royalty paid to the author, and sold at $1.50. Most of the remaining dollar went for distribution costs of the first edition, and then, as now, the publisher mostly made money on subsequent editions. The author's royalties ran from 10% to 20% of the retail price, and his or her share of the profits often amounted to twice what the publisher got. Publishers began to ask authors to accept a smaller royalty so they could bring out cheaper editions of books (Brett, 1913).

During the years that Perkins was an editor at Scribner's, 1910 until his death in 1947, publishing was in a very "personal period," in the words of one of his authors (Smith, 1962). Publishing houses were supported mostly by textbooks, mysteries, travel books, etc.; great works of literature were lucky if they covered their costs. The head editor, which was the title Perkins eventually gained, had a great deal of authority. According to Mr. Scribner, Perkins, like most editors in those days, would consult with colleagues and then make a decision. Royalties were smaller, advances were not nearly as important as they became later, and only a minority of authors had agents.

As for the writers, they went through their own changes between the wars: "The writers of the 1920s believed in everything, those of the 1930s in only one thing, those of the 1940s in nothing," as Hoffman (1955) describes them in his study of *The Twenties*.

In 1920, *Harper's* stated, "The writer who cannot find a publisher today either does not know how to write or has nothing to say that anyone cares to hear." Publishing shared in the boom of the decade. For the first time American literature became important. It was discussed constantly; writers and artists instantly became heroes. They went to live in Greenwich Village and Montparnasse, found odd jobs, mixed their own gin, rolled their own cigarettes, talked their way out of paying bills, wrote book and film reviews, and started first novels with the help of advances from hopeful publishers. Some were even able to support themselves by writing as soon as they left college (Brooks, 1965; Cowley, 1950; and Cunliffe, 1964).

These writers rebelled against the traditional forms of literature, and publishers gave in by paying attention to new, untried writers. As a generation they may have felt lost, but actually, said Cowley (1956), "They had an easy time of it: Hemingway, [Thornton] Wilder, [John] dos Passos, and Louis Bromfield were internationally known novelists before they were 30. They had a chance which the older men lacked to develop their craftsmanship in book after book; from the very first they were professionals."

By 1925, 15% became a maximum royalty at the end of a sliding scale. The standard was 10% on the first 2,500, 12½% on the next 2,500, and 15% after 5,000 (Cowley, 1954).

New publishers popped up almost as quickly as new writers: Harcourt Brace, Knopf, Viking, Random House, Farrar, Rinehart, Simon & Schuster. A lot of the publishing boom grew from phenomena such as Sinclair Lewis' *Main Street* in 1920, as Burlingame (1946) explains:

> In the year following its publication, it was number one on the bestseller list...It sold just under 300,000 in its first year. Critics wrote long articles trying to explain it by the public's new maturity, by post war "disillusionment" and a great fiction era was predicted...The lists did record at least one novel every year which even the sterner critics acclaimed as literature. This upset the old guessing-game in the editorial offices. No one could be sure any longer that a serious novel—even a somber, a tragic novel—might not become a bestseller.

What a time to be an editor. "It was a flower show of budding authors," says novelist Robert Nathan (in Berg, 1978). "To be an editor, I guess, was to be full of hope and excitement, and that feeling of not having enough hours in the day, because it sometimes seemed that everyone you met had a good book in him." They also felt part of the publishing houses with which they worked, "and felt they were making decisions for the company," notes Mr. Scribner.

After the 1929 stock market crash, publishing and the rest of the country stopped to take a breath, waiting for the young writers to grow and produce more mature works. Many publishers went bankrupt and sometimes the only writing jobs were on Henry

Luce's publications, such as *Time* and *Fortune*, allowing little time for writing first novels (Cowley, 1954).

The Federal Writers Project, established in 1936, created jobs, as did the movies, where almost anyone who had published a book could find work. "A writer's project retailored in mink," in Cowley's (1950) words. These writers had the same depressing view of the world and the future that the rest of society had in those days. Many began to idealize the Middle Ages (Brooks, 1965); even Fitzgerald, who had specialized in 1920s flappers, started work on a novel, *Phillippe, Count of Darkness*, about a French prince during the Crusades.

In the Depression there was "much fine writing born of desperation and survival," says McCormick (1962), "but with the beginning of World War II this spirit was lost, and editors had the new problem of trying to make writers write. The peak of this blight came between 1939-41, when the young writer said, 'How can I write when I don't know that there will be a world tomorrow?'"

In 1940 the average assistant in the production, advertising, or editorial end of a New York publishing house would earn anywhere from $18 to $70 per week, with an average of about $27. However, the union scale for compositors at that time was $54 per week, and as much as $65 for pressmen. Part of the difference is attributable to the large number of women in the editorial end of publishing (*Nation*, 1940).

By the end of that decade, the publisher was taking in three times as much revenue as 10 years before, but manufacturing costs were up 65%, and his "total inventory of mostly unwanted books piled in his warehouse may now amount to more than his capital and surplus together," noted Smith (1949). In Perkins' later days there were 2,000 professional writers earning money from books, but fewer than 100 did not need any other source of income (Cowley, 1944).

For a brief period at the end of World War II, writing became a profession that supported hundreds. The excess profits tax of wartime years encouraged magazines and motion picture studios to pay large sums for stories. The advances could be deducted from taxes, making the real cost of stories only a few cents on the dollar. Many publishers tried to reduce their excess profits by making advance payments for books that would not appear until the tax had been repealed (Cowley, 1954).

There was a different atmosphere on the staff of publishing houses then, says Mr. Scribner. There was less "restiveness," and the editor felt more of an obligation to the house than to his or her own career, agents, the public, or the profession. In 1947, the year Perkins died, three people retired from Scribner's with a total of 155 years with the company. In those days, "there was a tremendous continuity," said Mr. Scribner.

Scribner's

By the time Perkins arrived in 1910, Scribner's was one of the oldest, stodgiest houses in New York, with its own building on Fifth Avenue; its own successful magazine, *Scribner's* (which lasted until 1937); and equally successful bookstore. Their most prominent authors were John Galsworthy (*The Forsyte Saga*) and Edith Wharton (*The Age of Innocence*) (Burlingame, 1946; *Publisher's Weekly*, 1932; Madison 1966).

Charles Scribner's Sons was founded by the original Charles Scribner in 1846. When he died in 1871, there was a brief time when it was known as Scribner, Armstrong & Co., as a partnership which also published *St. Nicholas Magazine*, and later *Scribner's* magazine. In 1878, however, the firm was back in family hands, headed by Charles' three sons. Charles, Jr., known during the Perkins years as Old CS to everyone in publishing, became president and stayed in that position until he semi-retired to become chairman and his brother Arthur took over in 1928. Four years later, Arthur died and his nephew, Charles III, then 42, grandson of the original Charles, took over. During the war he brought his son Charles IV into the company, the Mr. Scribner whom I interviewed for this thesis. The company has since been bought by Simon and Schuster, and the Fifth Avenue bookstore is now owned by Barnes and Noble.

Charles Scribner, IV

In my 1980 interview, Mr. Scribner, who joined the firm in 1945, overlapping Perkins by two years, noted that as a small independent publishing house, Scribner's "was free of a lot of the rigidity" of larger concerns, giving Perkins more freedom. All the editors reported directly to Old CS, who personally signed the authors' contracts. All decisions on advances and royalties were "entirely ad hoc," although the editor had the final say on the design, production, promotion, etc. of the book. The only exception would be where there was a controversy over its acceptance, as there was with many of Perkins's early authors. Then the decision was made at the top and discussed at now famous editorial meetings. Editors at Scribner's, as at most houses, received no formal training, direction or guidance on how to do their jobs. It was "all by osmosis, all learning by doing," said Mr. Scribner.

When Arthur died suddenly and his nephew Charles succeeded him, in 1932, Perkins, 48, was promoted to editor-in-chief and vice-president of the company, taking on broader managerial responsibilities as well as his direct work with his authors. At that time he was in the midst of Fitzgerald's *Tender Is the Night*, Hemingway's *Death in the Afternoon* and Wolfe's *Of Time and the River* (Berg, 1978). According to Mr. Scribner, all the editorial employees at the company then were "from the same stratum of life...It was more like a law firm, genteel."

Scribner's was always a company of colorful personalities. The towering persona of the corporation was definitely Old CS, "a born publisher with great flair...who truly loved getting books into print," according to one of his editors, John Hall Wheelock (in Lynn, 1978). He is described as an "undisputed ruler," a "grandfather's image," (Berg, 1978) with a "wrath feared like Jehovah's" (Cowley, 1944). His younger brother Arthur was a Princeton man, and his nephew, the third Charles Scribner, was part of the New Jersey fox hunting set. When the younger Charles took over in 1932, there was a decided change in the office atmosphere from the days of Old CS, as Cowley (1944) describes:

> [The third Charles] had admired Fitzgerald and Hemingway from the beginning; also he liked to smoke in the office. All these changes, combined with the changing character of the list of authors, meant that Scribner's was losing its mid-Victorian atmosphere, ...reaching its low...when the office forces, arriving in the morning, would find Thomas Wolfe, after a night on the town, asleep on the director's table in the library.

Charles III was very close to Perkins, his contemporary, and had a great enthusiasm for the new literature they were publishing. Scribner's could boast other editors equally regarded by those in their profession—Edward Burlingame, editor of *Scribner's* magazine, whose son also worked for Scribner's and wrote the company's history; and William Cary Brownell, editor-in-chief before Perkins, "white-bearded and walrus-mustached, [who] had a brass spittoon and a leather couch in his office" (Berg, 1978). Perkins, who often worked standing up, and Burlingame, who sat on the edge of his chair, always marveled at Brownell's ability to read manuscripts lying down, but claimed that they did hear snoring coming from the room in the late afternoon (Burlingame, 1946).

Certainly, Scribner's was highly thought of, with or without Perkins. One of the few houses which had always been under the management of one family, it had a reputation for warm relations with authors, and Old CS was one of the fighters for international copyright laws. They owned their own press and bindery, one of the few general publishers who did then (Madison, 1966; Canfield, 1975; and Stern, 1942). The company was, in Mr. Scribner's words, in a position where it "could afford to be high-minded" about the books it published. They certainly did not have to build a list of books from nothing when Perkins arrived. "It was possible to take risks," said Mr. Scribner.

The house in those days is usually described as "tradition-encrusted" with a Dickensian atmosphere. The head accountant was in his 70s, perched on a high stool, poring over leather-bound ledgers (Berg, 1978). "No word unfit for a young girl's ear could appear in a book that Scribner's published," said Cowley (1944) of the pre-Perkins era. He pointed out that its book list seemed to be oblivious to the changes after World War I, including some of the emerging realists such as Theodore Dreiser, Sherwood Anderson or Carl Sandburg. Cowley (1944) has said that Perkins' coming made Scribner's take "a sudden leap from the age of innocence into the midst of the lost generation."

Mr. Scribner, however, felt that this view of the company as a buggy-whip factory being told to make automobile tires "makes a nice Hollywood scenario, but just isn't true." He acknowledged that Perkins did have a role in educating the other editors to "this type of writing," but it was not "contrary" to the type of books Scribner's had been publishing. "Scribner's had been publishing boldly before Perkins ever came," he told me. Despite the legendary effect of Hemingway's four-letter words on the staff, Mr. Scribner held that the company was not afraid of such words—"after all, they published them!"

Whatever the extent of the extremes, it is agreed that there was a decided change in the image of the house after Perkins began to have a say in the selection of books. Although he had great respect for the firm, as "he joined as an advertising copywriter not three years out of Harvard, Perkins was not intimidated," says Berg (1978). He was more inclined to take risks and began scouting out new authors. The house was not known, even in Perkins' heyday, for offering major advances. "When literary agents place important authors on the auction block, Scribner's is usually outbid," noted Cowley (1944). However, Perkins took chances on unknown writers, turned down by other houses.

Some felt that a lot of the spirit went out of the house when Old CS died, although Perkins was at the peak of his influence. As Lynn (1978) points out, "Neither Faulkner nor Steinbeck came to grace the Scribner's list—Perkins thought Faulkner was 'crazy'...In a caustic letter to Perkins in 1938, Edmund Wilson spoke of the 'general apathy and morbidity into which Scribner's seems to have sunk. You people haven't showed any signs of life since old man Scribner died.'"

Surely the general economic depression had its effect, too. In 1929, a big year for Scribner's, net earnings were almost $290,000; in 1932 they were a little under $41,000. Perkins had to tell all his authors that advances were tightening up even more (Berg, 1978).

Maxwell Perkins (1884-1947)

Although born in New York City in 1884, Maxwell Perkins is always credited with having strict New England traits. He came from a long line of Yankees and was graduated from Harvard University with a degree in economics in 1907. There he was greatly influenced by the legendary Professor Charles Townsend

Copeland, called Copey, whom he later edited and who instilled in him a love for literature. After graduation he worked for three years on the *New York Times* as a cub reporter, and then joined the firm of Scribner's, working in the advertising department until 1914. From that time until his death in June of 1947 he was an editor with the company, eventually achieving the titles of head editor and editor-in-chief (Knopf, 1950; Berg, 1978; Wheelock, 1950).

Perkins' office on Scribner's fifth floor has been described as "one of the most crowded cubbyholes," by one of his authors (Burt, 1951):

> Taking up most of the space was a big desk, stacked with books, manuscripts, and mail, neatly arranged. Everywhere were stacked books. On the walls, indiscriminately hung, were a few autographed photographs of authors, looking as though they had been put there and then forgotten. In one corner was a stiff-back chair for visitors—the corner nearest the door.

Perkins' best method, however, for keeping others' visits to his office short also became his trademark—he always wore his hat. An author had given him a "modest size, soft, fairly shapeless, and pearl gray" (Burt, 1951) sombrero which he wore back on his head, partly to make people think he was getting ready to leave but mostly to help his poor hearing. Eventually this hat gave way to others, but it seldom left his head in public (Weeks, 1950).

He usually entertained authors at his favorite lunch place, Cheerio's, where he was well-known and automatically served his favorite dish, beginning with martinis that would usually keep coming during lunch. Perkins also was known for making a perfunctory gesture to pay for the whole check, but managed to make his guest feel uncomfortable enough that he would volunteer to pay his share.

Perkins loved his work with such a passion that he wrote to a friend that he could see no reason not to do it seven days a week, saying of Sunday, "I hate it, and all other holidays, and also nights." He felt disappointed about books that he took on that did not sell or required more effort than they were worth to get to press (Berg, 1978).

> **Perkins' typical business day…**
>
> …began with reading correspondence, dictating letters to his secretary, and receiving callers. Later in the morning he would have informal editorial conferences with Old CS. In a 1935 letter to a close friend, he described a typical day which included:
>
> - answering a letter from an agent after skimming the proposed novel and asking to see more;
>
> - discussing with Old CS a book on the training of bird dogs which they decided to accept, and a new edition of [WB] Yeats' poetry;
>
> - talking to Wolfe's lawyer on the phone about some new evidence in their case against his former agent…;
>
> reading in the office late since he did not have to meet anyone for a late afternoon drink;
>
> - stopping to solve a minor problem with some advertising copy;
>
> - meeting in his office with the tennis champion Helen Wills Moody whose tennis…book they had published, confessing, "Helen Wills can't write" (Berg, 1978).

> **Perkins almost always took manuscripts home...**
>
> ...with him to read on the train. The actor Robert Ryan used to ride the train to Connecticut for some time and reported to Perkins' biographer, Berg:
>
> He always sat in the same corner seat of the train. He never took his hat off, you know...The rest of the world was just a blur to him. He plopped down without even looking around, then reached into his briefcase. For the next hour he just read. I noticed that he moved his lips when he read. He always looked a little lost...God, I never dared speak to him. Nobody did. Everybody noticed him, though he didn't notice us; but nobody wanted to bother him. You...might throw some poor writer's career in jeopardy (in Berg, 1978).

Perkins was known personally for his softness, in manner, in dressing, and in speech. He "would greet you with... [a] tight-lipped, bashful New England smile. He dresses in shabby and inconspicuous grays, as if he were trying not to be noticed," said Cowley (1944) in his *New Yorker* profile. The owner of Cheerio's said, "He like quiet. He never says one word unless you speak to him. He talk very delicate, very soft, and you won't want to miss a word" (in Berg 1978).

His voice, one of his distinctive characteristics, was "nasal, a trifle rasping, but quiet and well-bred; out of New England but with no trace of Harvard," as Burt (1951) describes it. Although very "approachable," in later years Perkins' silences were accentuated by forbidding grey-eyed stares that intimidated many of his authors. "That silence could on occasion be terrifying," said Wheelock (1950), "and when driven to desperation by some long-winded speaker, Max would sometimes puncture it with an irritable 'Well, what about it?'

which usually served to bring things to a head. He was not by any means always amiable."

Despite his best effort to remain anonymous, Perkins became a legend inside and outside his trade. During his peak years there was usually a Perkins book near the top of the bestseller list. In 1943 alone six Scribner's books were book-club choices. It is generally acknowledged that he had more volumes dedicated to him than any other person, as well as countless authors' acknowledgments. Cowley (1944) called him "the nearest thing to a great man now existing in the literary world." Many editors who knew him, talked to him on the phone, worked with him closely with certain authors, but never laid eyes on him in person (Berg, 1978).

Because of this legend, Perkins was, especially in later years, often forced to spend entire days answering the treaties of unknown authors, rejected authors, and untalented authors. Many would read over Wolfe's description of him as Foxhall Edwards in *You Can't Go Home Again*, looking for clues as to why he had turned them down.

Every analysis of Perkins' unique talent for working with writers begins or ends with an explanation of the conflicts in his background. Words such as "patrician," "granite" and "Yankee," describe his New England toughness, which conflicted with his "gentleness," "considerate" and "shy" side (Smith, 1962; Wheelock, 1950). "He combined loyalty to truth with a clairvoyant sense of what the public would like and buy," says one reviewer of his letters (Parsons, 1950). Berg (1978) says that the aestheticism he inherited from his father joined with the strong sense of discipline he got from his mother's side, giving him "artistic flair but New England common sense." His best friend, Van Wyck Brooks (1965), said that "one side appreciated the writers, the other side helped them, an ambivalence that explained why Max never became a writer himself and why he became the rock on which others leaned."

Berg (1978) also points out that "In some way...Perkins was unlikely for his chosen profession: He was a terrible speller, his punctuation was idiosyncratic, and when it came to reading, he was by his own admission, 'slow as an ox.'"

Perkins' only speaking engagement was to Ken McCormick's New York University (NYU) publishing class in 1946. McCormick talked Perkins into speaking by promising him, "a class of young hopefuls, and that excited him" (Berg, 1978). "Perkins had made a total impact. He showed his audience in the quietest way, without saying a word to polish his own literary reputation." One of the observers in that class noted, "His discourse quietly flowed as James Joyce would write. I kept thinking now and again of Charles Lamb. Max Perkins was ageless." Mr. Scribner summed him up by saying he "was a very kind man, with great sympathy, and understanding."

As a businessman, Perkins seems to have had a knack for knowing what the public liked (Epstein, 1978). Berg (1978) says of his business acumen:

> An over-tipper in restaurants and a soft touch to any friend or stranger who needed to borrow money; he was a Yankee mule trader in business. In discussing advances and royalties with agents or authors, Max would sit in silence at his desk, poker-faced, doodling his portraits of Napoleon, while the other person stated his demands. With his words falling on Perkins' almost deaf ears, even the toughest bargainer would gradually talk himself down. Old CS's grandson...said, "Max would close the deal whenever his terms were reached or his drawing was completed—whichever came first."

In business he was a conservative investor who managed to make substantial sums in the stock market by reinvesting his profits even during the worst months of the Depression (Berg, 1978).

One of the qualities most often mentioned in discussing Perkins is integrity. He has been described even by one of his critics as "a real gentleman" (Lynn, 1978). "You were ashamed to be disloyal to life or ideas when you were with Maxwell Perkins; unconsciously you did your best," said Burt (1951).

Another strong characteristic was tremendous humility, especially when faced with creative talent. He wrote to Marjorie Kinnan Rawlings, author of *The Yearling.* "I am always frightened to death of [speaking too definitely]. You must not take what I say as definite at all ever, but all as by way of example only" (in Parsons, 1950). Mixed with this humility was a large dose of tact. When asking for radical cuts in a manuscript, he would convince an author that the sections interfered with "the harmony of the narrative." Rawlings (1950) reports several of his authors agreed that "His special gift was his ability, as creative as that of the author himself, to understand what that writer was attempting to do and to say, to direct all criticism and all help toward that writer's own best expression, whether Max himself agreed or not." He truly meant it when he said in an early letter to Fitzgerald, "Do not ever defer to my judgment."

Most tellingly, he is credited with editing by suggestion rather than fiat. He had, said Pritchett (1973), "the art of discovering the passages where the novelist himself was uncertain and, without making overt suggestions, causing fruitful doubts to rise in his mind."

Wheelock (1950) cites an incident where an eminent critic was pointing out Wolfe's faults which he thought rendered all of Perkins' work worthless. The loyal editor flew into a rage: "Well, then you just don't care about talent!" He felt that a publisher's first allegiance was to talent. Scribner's policy, as he phrased it, was "to publish for an author rather than to publish individual works" (in Brown, 1950).

Cowley, in his profile, set down in order Perkins' rules for editing:

> When an author is sure of himself, the manuscript may go to the printer without a single comma shifted. Leave a writer's style alone, even if you don't approve of it. Make definite suggestions that are in the spirit of the author's intentions. Do not indulge your own suppressed creative instincts by changing the structure and meaning of other people's books. In a long, involved manuscript, try to bring order out of confusion. You must not be too meticulous. Aside from these commonplace rules his editing was inspired by his ability to discover what lay in the mind and heart of the writer. He never made abrupt suggestions, but in rambling conversations and observations slowly brought the writer to see his own errors. It might be called editing by osmosis (in Smith, 1947).

Perkins saw the editor in a position akin to that of one of the persons he most admired, Major General John Aaron Rawlin of General Ulysses S. Grant's staff. "It was his job to keep Grant sober; edit his important papers and put them in final form; apply tact and persistence in order to make critical points; and often restore the general's self-confidence," said Perkins (in Berg, 1978). He found it sad that a man became an editor because he loved books, "and then finds that he cannot possibly get time to read the books of any other publisher than the one he works for" (Cowley, 1944). Madeline Boyd, Wolfe's first agent, was probably one of many who asked him the question, "'Why don't you write yourself?' Max just stared at me for a long time," she later recalled, "and said, 'Because I'm an editor'" (Perkins, 1950).

Perhaps he described the role of the editor most eloquently in his address to the NYU publishing class. "An editor does not add to a book. At best he serves as handmaiden to an author. Don't ever get to feeling important about yourself, because an editor at most releases energy. He creates nothing" (in Berg, 1978).

Despite the paeans of praise raised to Perkins and his legend, he did have his limitations. Wheelock (1950) said his interest was in

> the development of American talent and literature. To the upcoming talents in countries other than his own, he was less than alert. Fiction was his principal concern...Scientific and abstract thinking interested him less than did books on controversial subjects or those based upon the application of a theory or idea. His passion was for the rare real thing, the flash of poetic insight that lights up a character or a situation and reveals talent at work. And his judgment was almost unerring in its clairvoyance.

When Perkins wanted to publish a work of non-fiction, it "tended to be crackpot," says Wheelock and towards the end "Max often became contrary and contradictory. Just plain Yankee stubborn" (in Berg, 1978). He was very rigid in his thinking in many ways, "schoolmasterish... [and] conventional," in Kazin's (1955) words, sometimes harping on certain ideas that he clung to against all evidence.

Perhaps the most serious criticism made about Perkins is his lack of knowledge of literature outside of that which he published. Perkins himself was quite candid about the inadequacy of his literary knowledge. "How frightfully ignorant I am in literature," he once explained to Hemingway, "where a publishing man ought not to be" (in Lynn, 1978).

But perhaps Perkins' special gift was even more basic: Charisma. In my discussion with Mr. Scribner, he summed up the Perkins charm in this way:

> This may sound like a lot of baloney, and you may think there's nothing to it. But I believe it's true. Perkins was

extraordinarily handsome. He had piercing blue-grey eyes and you would definitely notice him in a crowd. This gave him a sort of glamour, not in a Hollywood movie star sense...No one ever sassed him. You couldn't, he was so kind. He was like a gifted college professor. He was a help and an inspiration at the same time.

Relationship with Scribner's

Like Fayol, Perkins worked practically his entire life at one company, Scribner's. Except for his short stint as a *New York Times* reporter, and four and a half years in Scribner's advertising department, he spent his whole career as an editor. As advertising manager, Perkins made use of his "imagination (though no daring), an instinctive appreciation for the literary product, and a feel for what the public would buy," says Berg (1978). When one editor left to join another firm, Perkins was moved upstairs to the now famous fifth floor because Old CS was impressed with his work.

At first he spent most of his time proofreading galleys, correcting grammar in a gardening book or arranging the order of selections in anthologies. By 1923, while nurturing Fitzgerald and other young authors, he was feeling overwhelmed with the amount of work his job required, and asked for extra editorial help, which Old CS eventually provided. Scribner's was receiving 500 more manuscripts per year than they had just before World War I. Publishing was booming (Berg, 1978).

From 1918 to his peak as an editor in 1928, his salary doubled, to $10,000, and he was receiving substantial amounts of stock in the privately held company. Eventually his supervisor retired, meaning that Perkins had much more editorial freedom (Berg, 1978).

When Old CS died in 1930, Perkins was named a company officer and soon became editorial director. "After Scribner's death," says one of his co-workers, "Max really didn't have to defend his decisions any longer" (in Berg, 1978). When Arthur Scribner died two years later, and the younger Charles took over, Perkins was made vice president and given a corner office. In his profile, Cowley (1944) reported that a young author had asked him, "How did you ever start at Scribner's?" "Oh," Perkins said, "I've always been at Scribner's."

As a whole, Perkins's relationships with other employees of Scribner's were quite good. According to Mr. Scribner, sales conferences in Perkins' days were one-man shows where the editor rallied the sales force for his authors. One of the most important Scribner's people to Perkins and his authors was his secretary for almost the entire time he was there, Irma Wyckoff. "I don't know which of them should get more of the credit for the fact that Max always had time," says Smith (1962).

However, Perkins' other most important relationship within the company was with the president—Old CS, Arthur, or younger Charles. Most of his decisions, especially in the beginning of his career, were made in agreement with the president, including the amounts of royalties, advances, etc. All his recommendations were taken quite seriously, according to Mr. Scribner, "He was a colleague, not a subordinate of Old CS."

The younger editors at Scribner's knew that, if they had a new novelist they wanted Scribner's to publish, the best way to do it was to give the manuscript to Max (Berg, 1978). He had established himself in this role originally with the famous confrontation with the editorial board over Fitzgerald's first novel, *This Side of Paradise*, in 1919 after having been an editor for only five years.

Scribner's owed much of its financial success during these years to Perkins' decisions. After his successes with the early Fitzgerald and Hemingway books in the 1920s, he was listened to at editorial meetings. By 1926 he had acquired a remarkable list of writers for the firm. In the month that the stock market crashed,

Perkins brought out *A Farewell to Arms* and *Look Homeward, Angel* to overwhelmingly favorable critical and financial acclaim. Hemingway's sales reached 70,000 copies before the end of the year (Berg, 1978). These two classics, combined with other Perkins' novels, gave Scribner's their best year ever in 1930, the first year of the Depression.

> **Perkins was not always triumphant with Old CS...**
>
> ...and didn't always get him to agree to his projects. In particular, Perkins suggested publishing *The Man Nobody Knows*, a book which gave a Madison Avenue interpretation of the New Testament in 1925, depicting Christ as a salesman. Old CS was properly scandalized and turned it down against Perkins' protest that it would sell. When it became a runaway success, Scribner asked Perkins why they had not published it. Perkins reminded the forgetful Old CS that he had said it might sell and "the head of the company looked at Max a long time without a change of expression. With a faint twinkle in his eye, Scribner leaned forward, wagged his finger and said, 'But you didn't tell me, Mr. Perkins, that it would sell 400,000 copies'" (Berg, 1978).

Cowley (1944) pointed out in his *New Yorker* profile that Perkins was always an unconventional editor by any standards:

> He never attends [editor's] professional gatherings and he refuses to go to booksellers' conventions. He never accepts invitations to other publisher's cocktail parties or gives parties of his own to celebrate the publication of Scribner's books. He doesn't send notes to book reviewers telling them that something in his spring list is the greatest event since *Gone with the Wind*. He doesn't

invent plots for best-selling novels and call in his authors to write them. He doesn't ask literary agents for hot tips or look through magazines for new names. His authors say that he never talks to them about potential sales or movie rights.

These idiosyncrasies certainly kept his attention on what he felt was his real work, finding and encouraging talent. But this narrow focus did have some negative effects for the company in the long-run.

Toward the end of his career Perkins became less assertive with authors and the young editors followed suit by not pushing their authors as hard. "Max was passing up a number of obvious sure things," Mr. Scribner told me, "thereby missing out on good new authors." He said Perkins was taking chances on long shots because he could not bear to turn down long-time Scribner's authors. The new men at Scribner's felt that Perkins did not even want to listen to them. "At the editorial conferences, he hardly permitted any of the others to speak up. He presented all the prospective books, often in a manner which the fourth Charles Scribner described as 'Pickwickian in the extreme.' [Charles] felt that Perkins was overloading the list with second rate fiction, and was not alert to the country's new hunger for non-fiction" (Berg, 1978).

By the 1940s, Wolfe had deserted him; Fitzgerald died in 1940 at age 44 without having made a public comeback, but perhaps on the brink of his greatest work. Hemingway had produced *Bell*, which turned out to be the last great novel by one of Perkins' triumvirate.

By this time Perkins would sign up authors and then try to convince them to write books that had been pet projects of his, such as "a historical narrative to show how intelligence, in times of crisis, is almost always overcome, and, tragically, by emotion"

(Berg, 1978). In his later years he drank heavily, perhaps even in his office, according to Mr. Scribner.

McCormick, after hearing Perkins address his class,

> sat alone in the empty room and thought of something Booth Tarkington had once said...about how difficult it had become for him to respond to the writing in books he read. "I know all the tricks," Tarkington remarked; he had spent so many years performing them himself. "In that same way," said McCormick, "I felt that Max knew all the tricks of his trade and he had grown weary" (Berg, 1978).

After Perkins' death, Scribner's was left with a gap to fill, as any company would be after losing an employee who had been so important for so long. There were few close contacts with agents, because of Perkins' style of working directly with authors and this was another area that had to be re-built. Mr. Scribner says that the worst effect was the lop-sidedness of their list—"Too much fiction." He felt that the company had to get back "in the mainstream of publishing."

Relationships with Authors

Looking at the way Perkins worked with all his authors, we can see the general management principles of good supervision. One of his writers points out that it was his business to help authors. "If he had gone around getting authors upset it would have been bad for business" (Hale, 1968).

In his own writing, mostly letters, Perkins often described his feelings about creative people, always in the most positive tones. He felt it was important for his authors to stay flexible, un-self-conscious, as when he wrote to James Jones, "A deft man may toss his hat across the office and hang it on a hook if he just naturally does it, but he will always miss if he does it consciously." He also wrote to Jones about one of the criteria he used for defining someone as a writer:

> I remember reading somewhere what I thought was a very true statement, to the effect that anybody could find out if he was a writer. If he were a writer, when he tried to write, out of some particular day, ...that he could recall exactly how the light fell and how the temperature felt, and all the qualities of it. Most people cannot do it. If they can do it, they may never be successful in a pecuniary sense, but ability is at the bottom of writing (in Berg, 1978).

Contrary to Fayol's dictum about communicating verbally rather than in writing, Perkins wrote prolifically to his authors, in letters or memoranda, often "by hand where the situation was delicate and it was desirable to give a letter a more personal and intimate touch," according to Wheelock (1950).

One of his other more overt techniques was passing out copies of Leo Tolstoy's *War and Peace* like the "Gideon's dispense Bibles," in Berg's (1978) words. "I've made a lot of trouble for writers—and for myself—by getting them to read *War and Peace*," he wrote to a friend.

He also picked up a habit that cost him time as his legend grew. After Cowley's (1944) *New Yorker* piece stated that Perkins' "judgment depends on the person rather than the manuscript," the editor was besieged by young unknowns wanting to have just a few minutes with him so they could show their stuff.

Perkins' relationships with authors were also characterized by tremendous loyalty and he expected loyalty in return. Mr. Scribner points out that he understood authors' needs, financial and spiritual, and was generous to them, "out of loyalty and because they were terribly talented writers," even making advances out of his own pocket. Most important, he stuck by them despite, not because of, their success or failure. There was a legend among agents at the time that Perkins' authors didn't hit their stride and become financially successful until their third novel (Cowley, 1944).

Perkins felt that, as disparate as all his authors were, the one thing they had in common was lack of self-confidence when working on a book, as he told Rawlings:

> "They do have a subconscious confidence...But when they begin a big piece of work they have vastly less confidence...I wish I could give you that, for I am sure you could make it a lovely book, and full of the truth of life...I only hope that what I've said in this letter...may give you an idea, and not that you will follow it closely, but that it will suggest a way" (Perkins, 1950).

"The process is so simple," he told the NYU publishing class. "If you have a Mark Twain, don't try to make him into a Shakespeare or make a Shakespeare into a Mark Twain. Because in the end an editor can get only as much out of an author as the author has in him" (in Berg, 1978). Mr. Scribner described Perkins's technique as "a marvelous understanding of what these writers were doing and [he] had a great rapport with them." He always made the writers feel that any of their troubles or problems were not small or trivial, down to taking care of the sick cat of one persistent female writer.

Perkins' true medium for managing his writers was suggestion. He had a very clear knack for making suggestions so that the author thought he or she had come up with the idea. His comments, said Davenport, "were effective almost subliminally; he had a way of gently tossing them out as one would pebbles into a pond, making rings of meaning which enlarged until they touched the author's consciousness" (in Berg, 1978).

When an author was sure about what was to be done, he made very few if any grammatical or punctuation changes, seeing these as "unimportant details." But the big book that had gotten into a big mess was a Perkins dream, for he could unravel the problem with just the right word or question (Cowley, 1944).

He gave these suggestions both in person and in writing, saying often, "I hope this gets over to you. If I saw you for 10 minutes I know you would understand and would agree with me" (in Hale, 1968). In his letters he often commented on certain elements or episodes in a novel and gave detailed plans for its reorganization.

Often the best advice Perkins gave to his authors was to do nothing. "Turning things over in your mind, and reflecting upon them...is something that a writer ought to have to do in quiet circumstances" he wrote to one (Perkins, 1950).

In person his suggestions seem to mostly be characterized by great lapses of conversation and looks from sea-gray eyes. "The most important obligation of friendship is to listen," he wrote to one of his daughters. Perkins would become particularly fidgety if authors began to discuss their personal problems, however. "He would look away in embarrassment and fuss with his hearing aid, and when I paused he would interrupt me," says Smith (1962). Smith also describes a typical lunch in which he, the author, is proposing an idea to Perkins:

> Generally the communication through the first drink, and often for long minutes after, was silence and a good deal of telepathy flashing off those glances of Max's grey eyes. I usually knew before anything was said whether he approved or disapproved whatever I had proposed...Max would break his silence and his stare by speaking directly to the question...his manner would be argumentative, sometimes pleading, with quick gestures and eyebrows lifted high for emphasis. If the matter were important, like a new book I wanted to start, and we didn't agree after the second drink, we had a third. If we didn't agree then, we had a fourth and if we didn't agree then, we had another lunch. When we reached agreement, we walked

back to the office and Max gave me a check... [The first and perhaps second time] he disappeared and came back with Arthur or Charles Scribner's signature on my bread and butter. But for at least our last three books, Max sat down at his desk, wrote and signed the check himself as vice president of the firm.

> **Ponderous silences have different effects on different authors...**
>
> ...Burlingame recalls a time when a writer was in Perkins' office telling of his terrible problems:
>
>> Perkins went to the window as if overcome by the burden of his sympathy, and gazed down to Fifth Avenue. After a few moments of surveying the street, rocking slightly, he appeared ready to speak, and the writer waited in anticipation for his editor's comment on his plight. "You know," said Perkins without turning, "I can't understand why all these busy people move so slowly. The only ones who move fast are the boys on roller skates who have nothing to do. Why don't we—why doesn't everybody—wear skates?" The writer later gave Perkins credit for thoroughly distracting him from his problem (Berg, 1978).

Another Scribner's colleague reports that at one luncheon with an author who laid out all his problems on the table, "Max ate slowly, not saying a word. Toward the end of the meal, which lasted several hours, the writer rose from the table, grabbed the editor's hand with both of his, spluttered, 'Thank you, Mr. Perkins, for all your help,' and bolted out the door" (Berg, 1978).

The editor must hand out criticism as well as praise. "His objections, his criticisms," according to Hale (1968), "are always wrapped in an identification with the author's point of view. Perkins never tells these writers to be different from the way they are; he seems to be telling them how to become even more themselves...It is as if he accepted the work under consideration with a heartfelt 'yes!' and then, and only then, added, 'But...!'"

In rejecting authors he did not always, as is usually thought, practice "author soothing," as in "We love your idea but right now it just doesn't fit into our list." Instead, as Smith (1962) explains, "Max's method with but one swift needle-prick of pain, was cleaner and the inoculation was permanent." Smith also points out that his praise was only given in hints and teases as well, "His expression of approval...rarely got more exuberant than the little private smile, alternating with the appraising glare, and perhaps a shift of position in his chair, showing emotion."

But, the more he knew an author, the more demonstrative became Perkins' disapproval. Smith (1962) remembers four grades of it:

> First, if the matter were slight, there was a simple, good-natured scowl, perhaps with little shakes of the head, all not more than a social mannerism related to small talk. Second, if the matter really got into his attention, there was the censorious or appraising version of the gray-eyed stare, but alleviated by the little smile as if to say he knew you were too intelligent to be serious about anything so silly. Third, there was the censorious stare unrelieved by the smile, very stately and terrible. And fourth, if you proposed something intolerable that could not be ignored, the stare was reinforced along the fine nose by the lift of a scornful nostril in olfactory discomfort, to which might be added a nauseous smile that was trying unsuccessfully to be forbearing. It was an expression of horrified compassion that you, his friend, his author—

and therefore a very great author!—should have fallen into this dreadful delusion. The expression would last a few seconds, which was sufficient eternity then it would resolve into a scowl and scatter in small negative headshakes. But those seconds were plenty. Not only did the passage persuade me that the notion had been imbecile, but it threw me in turn into compassion for him, poor Max, poor very God, that I, in my childish blindness, should have imposed.

Influence

Perkins' influence on the company he worked for was not 100% positive. Besides his effect on their reputation and profits, which was positive, and on their company policy, which was mixed, his legend also influenced the other editors. Mr. Scribner pointed out that many sat in their offices waiting for the next Wolfe to come walking through their doors with a carton of classic under one arm. As a result many became "too deferential to authors," which "induced an atmosphere of timidity." They were afraid to ask their writers to try something new or begin a new book, and, Mr. Scribner said, they "should have been more assertive of our needs."

One of Perkins' accomplishments was to leave behind a large number of books which are not only literary classics but also popular best sellers. As Berg (1978) says, "Perkins was certain that the immortal books addressed themselves to the literate and the masses alike. 'The great books,' he said, 'reach both.'" In his obituary in the *New York Times* (1947) he was credited with earning his reputation on two levels: "On the one hand, his shrewd discernment of the worth of new writers and his advice to them developed unknowns to greatness; on the other his telling judgment on manuscripts produced scores of best sellers."

At the time of his death, much of his powers and skills, though not his influence, had waned. Smith (1962) recalls that "I never attended a funeral where there were more writers than went out to New Canaan [CT] for Max's...Those authors had lost something strong, like a personal god, and they knew it could not be replaced." Mr. Scribner recalls that "when he died people were talking about it in the subways as if it were Babe Ruth."

Photo Gallery of Other Perkins' Authors

Ring Lardner (1885-1933)

Ring Lardner is now best known for his humorous sports essays and his son, Ring Lardner, Jr., Oscar-winning scriptwriter of *M*A*S*H*. Lardner was on the fringes of the Algonquin Round Table, but in the center of partying and drinking on Long Island with Fitzgerald, who recommended him to Scribner's. Perkins pushed him to publish collections such as *How to Write Short Stories* (1925), but never convinced him to write a novel, despite constant nudging.

Marcia Davenport (1903-1996)

Perkins published weak books from Marcia Davenport before her second novel, *Valley of Decision*, about a Pittsburgh manufacturing family. Davenport put Perkins' letter of suggestions on one side of her typewriter, the manuscript on the other, and got to work. *Valley of Decision* was a critical and financial success, as a novel and an Oscar-winning film with Gregory Peck and Greer Garson. Perkins encouraged her next, *East Side, West Side*, about her life in Manhattan, which was also a hit novel and TV series with George C. Scott.

Marjorie Kinnan Rawlings (1896-1953)

Working with Marjorie Kinnan Rawlings through two weak novels about her earlier social life in New York, Perkins urged her to write about north Florida where she lived: "A book about a boy and the life of the scrub is what we want" (Perkins, 1950). So she sat down and wrote the classic *The*

Yearling. Rawlings was portrayed in the film based on her memoir, *Cross Creek*, by Mary Steenburgen; a visiting Perkins was played by Steenburgen's then husband, Malcolm McDowell, although in reality the editor and writer rarely met.

Sherwood Anderson (1876-1941)

Sherwood Anderson was an Ohio businessman who became the first of the American ex-patriate writers to visit Gertrude Stein's in Paris. He brought Hemingway to his own publisher, Boni & Liveright, but like Hemingway, switched to Perkins at Scribner's. One of the few Perkins' authors to feel neglected by his editor, Anderson moved to Harcourt, Brace. He died age 64 of peritonitis from eating a canapé with a toothpick in it.

James Jones (1921-1977)

James Jones stubbornly brought his first novel personally to Perkins' office in the mid-1940s, determined to wait until the legendary editor showed up. After mentioning that his second book might be about the peacetime army just before Pearl Harbor, Perkins gave him a $500 advance (Berg, 1978). Jones' manuscript for *From Here to Eternity* was on the editor's bed table when he was dying. It was published by Scribner's in 1951.

Alan Paton (1903-1988)

Alan Paton's South African novel, *Cry, the Beloved Country*, was one of the manuscripts next to Perkins' bedside when he was taken to the hospital. Paton only worked with him near the end of the editor's life, and found him to be a bit confused and rambling during a drinking lunch.

Erskine Caldwell (1903-1987)

Although Erskine Caldwell's first Scribner's book was a short story collection that didn't sell, Perkins still brought out his first novel, *Tobacco Road* (1932). It didn't do well, but the play and film versions were hits. After switching publishers, Caldwell wrote, "The one and only time Maxwell Perkins took me to lunch, he ordered for each of us a peanut butter and jelly sandwich and a glass of orange juice" (Caldwell, 1950).

Erskine Caldwell described an encounter with Perkins...

...soon after he began his writing career. Determined to break into <u>Scribner's</u> magazine, he sent the stories to Perkins, rather than through the magazine editor (Berg, 1978). Caldwell dropped off the stories without seeing Perkins, but got a phone call from him later, which Caldwell related this way:

[MP]: I got your manuscript yesterday...I wish you had asked for me when you were here...By the way, I've read all your stories on hand now...and I don't think I need to see any more for a while.

[EC]: (Silence.)

[MP]: I think I wrote you some time ago that we want to publish one...

[EC]: I received your letter. You haven't changed your mind, have you? I mean about taking a story?

[MP]: Changed my mind? No. Not at all. The fact is that we're all in agreement here at the office...I guess so much so that we've decided now to take two stories...and run them both in the magazine at the same time...How much do you want for the two together? We always have to talk about money sooner or later....Would 250 be all right? For both of them...

[EC]: 2.50? I don't know. I thought maybe I'd receive a little more than that.

[MP]: You did? Well, what would you say to 350 then? That's about as much as we can pay, for both of them. In these times...we have to watch our costs...

[EC]: I guess that'll be all right. I'd thought I'd get a little more than three dollars and a half, though, for both of them.

[MP]: $3.50? Oh, no! I must have given you the wrong impression, Caldwell. Not three dollars and a half. No, I meant $350.

[EC]: You did! Well, that's sure different. It sure is (in Berg, 1978).

IV

Maxwell Perkins and F. Scott Fitzgerald, Ernest Hemingway and Thomas Wolfe

"[Perkins] did the least for Hemingway, the most for Wolfe, and, despite his generous devotion, was unable to save Fitzgerald from himself. In Fitzgerald, Hemingway and Wolfe, Perkins had a boozer, a bully and a baby; even for writers, these three were very shaky hombres" (Epstein, 1978).

It can be argued that the only thing these three had in common as writers was their American heritage and Maxwell Perkins. Fitzgerald acknowledged their kinship when he wrote to Perkins from Hollywood, just before Wolfe's death, "What a time you've had with your sons, Max—Ernest gone to Spain, me gone to Hollywood, Tom Wolfe reverting to an artistic hillbilly" (Fitzgerald, 1963a).

The three differed in their work habits as well, as Cowley (1954) points out:

Wolfe wrote everything with pen or pencil, then had his manuscripts copied. Fitzgerald used the same method, but not for the reason Wolfe gave, that his hands were too big for the keyboard of a typewriter. Hemingway types his short stories but does the first drafts of his novels in pencil, counting the words at the end of each writing day. "If you write with a pencil," he says, "You get three different sights at it to see if the reader is getting what you want him to. First when you read over it; then when it is typed you get another chance to improve it, and again in proof."

Particularly in their response to criticism, Perkins knew their differences. Sadleir (1950) noted that the editor could rely on Fitzgerald's response to his suggestions as "considered and malleable." Wolfe in contrast, "was a savage tangle of diffidence, suspicion, and, when the climax came, of ungrateful brutality. His sensitivity to criticism was pathological." Berg (1978) points out that Hemingway protested too much about how indifferent he was to critics, but Wolfe ranted and raved and could spend "months in silent torment."

For Fitzgerald Perkins was a personal adviser, father figure and friend, but also a continual source of his only strength at times, financial and moral. For Hemingway, Perkins was dutifully in awe of "the Hemingway mystique of the big game hunter and general sportsman," in Berg's (1978) words. "For Wolfe he was the father-figure, and probably his only true, close friend. The downfall of their relationship was that too many people also saw him as Wolfe's co-author," said Berg (1978).

Because they are such different writers in style and temperament, an analysis of how Perkins worked with each of them is the best way to determine the basic principles behind his management technique.

F. Scott Fitzgerald

F. Scott Fitzgerald was the first major writer Perkins discovered, edited and helped.

Fitzgerald was born in Minneapolis, MN, in 1896, attended prep school and Princeton University back East, leaving college without officially graduating. He entered the Army in World War I, but wasn't sent overseas, and he met Zelda Sayre, the belle of Montgomery, AL, while stationed there. She would not marry him until he had the prospect of being wealthy, so he started writing a novel. Weeks after *This Side of Paradise* was published by Scribner's, he and Zelda married and became very famous very quickly. In the twenties they were idolized in the media as the golden couple of the Jazz Age, and he sold stories to the *Saturday Evening Post* at $4,000 a shot. He described the wild life on Long Island in the 1920s in *The Great Gatsby*, the life of the expatriates on the Riviera in the 1930s in *Tender Is the Night*, and was beginning to get back on his feet and capture the life of Hollywood in *The Last Tycoon* when he died of a heart attack in 1940. Perhaps because his life uncannily paralleled the mood of the country from 1920 to 1940, Fitzgerald's career is often seen as the archetypal tale of an author who suffered for his art, and never made enough money to live in what he thought was style. Zelda, a novelist and dancer, eventually succumb to their frenetic lifestyle and was hospitalized for the last years of her life in a sanitarium. She died there in a fire in 1948 (Berg, 1978; Graham and Frank, 1958; Mizener, 1974; Turnbull, 1962; and other sources).

A Hollywood restaurateur, commenting on Fitzgerald's death, said, "Scott Fitzgerald was a failure as a success—and a failure as a failure" (in Bruccoli, 1978). However, in the peak 20 years of his career, he published four novels, a play, more than 160 short stories, a score of essays, and left an unfinished major novel at his death. In *The Autobiography of Alice B. Toklas*, Gertrude Stein proclaimed, much to the chagrin of serious critics that "Fitzgerald would be read when all the others are forgotten" (in Hatcher, 1935).

Fitzgerald's entire oeuvre was published by Scribner's and edited by Perkins.

Fitzgerald's Major Works
His novels were:
This Side of Paradise (1921)
The Beautiful and Damned (1922)
The Great Gatsby (1925)
Tender Is the Night (1934)
The Last Tycoon, edited with notes by Edmund Wilson, unfinished, published posthumously (1941).

He also published four books of short stories:
Flappers and Philosophers (1921)
Tales of the Jazz Age (1922)
All the Sad Young Men (1926)
Taps at Reveille (1935)
And one play:
The Vegetable (1923), which had a short, unsuccessful run.

Fitzgerald's earnings from writing, his main source of income, reflect the ups and downs of his career. In 1919, before he published *Paradise,* he earned $879 from the sale of a few articles and his Army pay. In 1921, his first year as a successful novelist, he earned $18,850, increasing to $19,065 the following year. After his second book appeared, his earnings rose to $25,135, and went up again the next year, 1923, to $28,760. This increase continued, reaching its peak in 1931, six years after *Gatsby,* but before *Tender,* with annual earnings of $37,599, a phenomenal sum in the midst of the Depression (Turnbull, 1962; Donaldson and Donaldson, 1980; Bruccoli, 1972).

However, eight years later, in 1939, nine of his books were in print but his total royalties on them amounted to $33.71. Fitzgerald kept scrupulous records of his income up until 1931 when he stopped itemizing his earnings from individual works because the sums were so small. None of Fitzgerald's books ever made the top ten best seller list, and, in 1926, the height of the twenties, the Lost Generation writers were not represented by a single book in the top ten. Ernest Hemingway did not appear in this list until 1940 when *For Whom the Bell Tolls* was in fourth place (Turnbull, 1962; Donaldson and Donaldson, 1980; Bruccoli, 1972).

An integral part of Fitzgerald's relationship with Perkins was both their relationships with Hemingway. Fitzgerald recommended the younger writer to Scribner's and became close friends with him in Paris in the 1920s. Their friendship waned as his fame declined and Hemingway's increased. Despite many cruel moves on Hemingway's part, Fitzgerald always looked up to him and his talent. Even during the period when they were estranged as friends, and most of their communication was taking place through Perkins, "Scott had always expressed, both to Ernest and about him to others, the same unstinted enthusiasm for his work that had impelled him to bring Hemingway to Scribner's attention," said Esquire editor Arnold Gingrich (1966).

Work Habits

Despite his heavy drinking, Fitzgerald was rigidly disciplined as a writer. An analysis of his stories shows that the banal plots about flappers are most often expressed in words which "show the same careful attention to verbal tonalities as his best novels," as Prigozy (1971) says. Bruccoli (1963) found that "The stories reveal themselves as the equivalent of a more orderly writer's notebooks...Fitzgerald frequently experimented with themes, characters and settings that he subsequently developed in his novels. Bits of descriptions were often removed from a story, polished, and then inserted into a novel." Analysis of the story manuscripts shows layers of revision, whereas in his novels, he often rewrote in the galleys. Bruccoli's analysis of the many versions of *Tender* show that he rarely reorganized paragraphs, and even less often changed meaning. But, "he was endlessly patient about trying to make a sentence more graceful or striking" (Bruccoli, 1978).

One of Fitzgerald's secretaries said that, in the most depressed period of his career, he wrote stories three or four times each, but started each new version with a clean typewritten draft. When asked about this habit, he explained, "Yes, three drafts are absolutely necessary. First, the high inspirational points. Second, the cold going over. Third, putting both in their proper perspective" (in Turnbull, 1962).

Fitzgerald's partner in Hollywood, Sheilah Graham, said that he always spoke of his writing very seriously, never disparaging it or making jokes (Graham and Frank, 1958). When Zelda was in psychotherapy, her doctor wanted Fitzgerald to also undergo psychotherapy as treatment for his drinking problem. Fitzgerald was dead set against it. Part of his refusal came from pride, but part was from "the artists' instinctive distrust of having his inner workings tampered with," in the words of Turnbull (1962). "He was afraid that the psychiatric treatment might make him a reasoning, analytic person, instead of a feeling one, and he instanced several novelists who had been psychoanalyzed and had written nothing but trash ever since."

Fitzgerald was fastidious about not using phrases more than once, making preparation of his last short story collection, *Taps at Reveille*, harder than any of the others. The stories chosen had been "stripped and bled" for passages used in *Tender*. After all the revisions to the novel, Fitzgerald could not remember what he had left in and what had come out. He spent months going through the novel looking for phrases he had already used. To Perkins' objections, Fitzgerald replied,

> One of [my virtues] happens to be a great sense of exactitude about my work...This is in no way a question of laziness. It is a question of absolute self-preservation...Certain people I know read my books over and over again and I can't think of anything that would more annoy or disillusion a reader than to find an author using

a phrase over and over, as if his imagination were starving (in Berg, 1978).

Although Fitzgerald viewed his talent as fragile, as capital which could easily be wasted, he knew that it also represented his only power. He told his secretary, "I can be so tender and kind to people in even little things, but once I get a pen in my hand, I can do anything." He cautioned a fellow dejected writer that it was impossible to write on demand for magazines' needs. Even when he desperately needed money, he instructed his agent to tell the editor of the *Post*, "pleasantly of course, that I just can't work that way—still there's no use telling him—the harm's done but if he has any other ideas about writing stories, please don't tell me" (in Turnbull, 1962; Fitzgerald, 1963b; Fitzgerald and Ober, 1972).

Novelist Morley Callaghan (1963) reports that during the summer he spent with the Fitzgeralds in Paris, he described how he felt about his chosen career:

> He had to write eight stories a year for the *Saturday Evening Post* at $4000 a story. Oh, so I thought $4000 a story was a lot of money, eh? Well, in view of the value of the storywriter to the big circulation magazines, he was actually being underpaid. [He] had to be always looking around for material for those eight stories...Yet he also had to find time to turn to the work that was the core and hope of his whole life—his novel... My God, there was never enough time. And when he found this time he couldn't seem to tap his imagination at will...He argued sensibly that any man who had an income of $50,000 a year [as he did] was a millionaire...Our confusion came from suspecting he didn't have a million dollars in capital. We were right. But we were overlooking the fact that a writer's capital was the writer's talent. [which] brought him in $50,000 a year, very well, then wasn't he to be ranked as a millionaire?

Fitzgerald, in comparison to Hemingway and in strong contrast to Wolfe, took suggestions, advice and criticism well. He wrote to Hemingway working on *The Sun*: "I've taken what proved to be excellent advice (on *The Beautiful and Damned*) from Bunny Wilson who never wrote a novel, on *Gatsby* (—change of many thousand words) from Max Perkins who never considered writing one, and on *This Side of Paradise* from Katherine Tighe...who had probably never read a novel before" (in Bruccoli, 1978). Callaghan (1963) found that he avidly read all his reviews. "He read them carefully. No, it wasn't a waste of time. There was always the chance that some reviewer, even missing the point, might make one helpful remark." But, five or six years later, as the reviews got worse, he wrote to his agent, Harold Ober, "Don't send me any more gloomy reviews... Unfavorable criticism upsets me these days—always has" (in Fitzgerald and Ober, 1972).

Bruccoli (1978) found that

> the crucial difference was in the public images Fitzgerald and Hemingway projected. Hemingway radiated confidence and dedication. Everything he did seemed to relate to his work. Fitzgerald, who had an abysmal sense of literary public relations, became a symbol for dissipation and irresponsibility. As Hemingway recognized, at some point in the late 1920s, Fitzgerald seemed to enjoy [failure]...He knew how good he was: geniuses always know.

In his last Hollywood days, those closest to him watched his talent, his perception of it, and his perception of himself, deteriorate. The most telling story of how he worked during his last period is told by author Catherine Drinker Bowen:

> I...found Harold [Ober] at his desk, reading manuscript and looking depressed... He passed me some typed sheets and asked what I could make of them. The pages were

interlined, written over in red ink, blotched, almost illegible, and made no sense at all. Harold said that was the way Scott's stories had been coming in lately...I think it was as though one of his own sons had defected and gone past the point of no return (in Bruccoli, 1972).

Relationship with Perkins

In a letter to Perkins before the publication of *Paradise*, Fitzgerald wrote, "I feel I've certainly been lucky to find a publisher who seems so generally interested in his authors. Lord knows this literary game has been discouraging enough at times" (in Berg, 1978). Unlike many authors and editors Fitzgerald and Perkins remained close friends throughout Fitzgerald's career, each always showing total respect for the other's talents.

Fitzgerald required less help than Wolfe, yet more than Hemingway. Most of Perkins' assistance was passed along through letters and telegrams no matter where Fitzgerald was living. Despite Fitzgerald's at times debauched lifestyle, certainly alien to Perkins's upbringing, his constant request for funds, and the long stretches with no viable work, Perkins never reproached him and never lectured him on morality. In the darkest years of Fitzgerald's career, only Perkins and his wealthy neighbor from the Riviera, Gerald Murphy, remained his friends. Critics have theorized that Perkins lived vicariously thru Fitzgerald's escapades, and many have called him a surrogate father (Kuehl and Bryer, 1971). Berg (1978) sees it more as the relationship between "a rather stiff but indulgent uncle—Max liked to surprise Scott with small gifts...to a spoiled, dashing, irresistible nephew."

The initial reason, of course, for Perkins and Fitzgerald to come together was business. As with many of his authors, they had no written contract because, as he explained in the beginning, "It might be right for you sometime to change publishers, and while this would be a tragedy to me, I should not be so small as to stand in the way on personal grounds" (in Fitzgerald and

Perkins, 1971). Perkins supervised the production of all of Fitzgerald's books, even after the author's death.

Money

One of the bases of the friendship and business relationship between Perkins and Fitzgerald was the former's willingness to lend enormous amounts of money to the latter when in need—which was often. Mr. Scribner said that the advances were "extreme in terms of needs and extreme in terms of [Fitzgerald's] talents." They were not only from Scribner's, but also from Perkins' own pocket.

Fitzgerald's career is tinged throughout with enormous amounts of, or lack of, money. He never had what he felt was enough even when he was making more than any other American author. Indeed, back in his Princeton days, Fitzgerald was already musing on the basic conflict, "to write either books that would sell or books of permanent value. He was not sure at the time which he should do. He never decided" (Berg, 1978).

Soon after the publication of *Paradise*, Fitzgerald was writing Perkins that he had $6,000 worth of bills, he owed his literary agent $600 for an advance on a story which he was not able to write, and his bank would no longer lend him money on the security of his stock. He asked for the first of many advances on his next novel, in progress, and Perkins got $1,600 for him from Scribner's. In a few months, he was again short $1,000 because of income taxes, and Perkins reminded him that he still had more than that coming to him from royalties (Berg, 1978).

Early on Perkins had told Fitzgerald to request money whenever he needed it, and the young author took him at his word. He asked for $1,500 because his wife needed a new fur coat. By the end of the first year, he had received more than $5,000 in advance against future earnings, and lost track of how many times he had asked for money (Berg, 1978).

In May of 1921, Perkins made his promise to Fitzgerald in writing, stating

> We shall always be ready to advance, not only amounts equivalent to what your books have already earned, although payment may not then be due, but amounts which may be considered reasonable estimates of what it may be anticipated they will earn. In other words, the only reason why we are not making you a very handsome advance is that the figure is perhaps a little difficult to fix on, but chiefly because we thought that…an arrangement by which you were free to draw against your account here and reasonably in excess of it, would be more convenient and satisfactory (Fitzgerald and Perkins, 1971).

This arrangement was in line with Fitzgerald's spend-it-now philosophy of life. There is at least one letter written by Fitzgerald to Perkins, in 1922, in which he did not beg, saying instead, "I'm sure you skipped to the end to see if I wanted money—but for once I don't" (Fitzgerald, 1980).

Although his second book, *The Beautiful and Damned*, did well, Fitzgerald was in debt to Scribner's because of the advances. He asked if he could assign the royalty payments from his play-in-production, *The Vegetable*, to them. He needed $650 in the bank by the next Wednesday or "I'll have to pawn the furniture…I don't even dare come up there personally but for God's sake try to fix it." Perkins arranged to have the money deposited without assigning the royalties, and the play was not a success (Berg, 1978). When sent a new royalty report, Fitzgerald invariably asked for a new loan, keeping him always behind in his debt to the publisher.

From *Gatsby* (1925) to *Tender* (1934) was one of the most trying times in Fitzgerald's career. His wife's mental illness worsened and they wandered from Europe to the States and back again. Perkins confided to Hemingway that Scribner's had advanced so much to Fitzgerald that he did not see how he could possibly pay it back, even if the next novel was an enormous hit. Eventually, half of Zelda's small royalties from her novel, *Save Me the Waltz*, were assigned against her husband's bill (Berg, 1978). In the midst of depressions and financial slides, Fitzgerald wrote to Perkins after a quick visit to New York, "In the usual confusion of leaving your city, I don't know whether I paid my bill at the Algonquin, whether you paid it, or whether it was paid at all. Have you got any dope on the subject?" Perkins paid it (in Fitzgerald, 1980).

Fitzgerald also received innumerable advances from his literary agent, Ober, perhaps more than from Perkins personally, at a time when Ober was just setting up his business and putting his children through school (Berg, 1978). In the mid-thirties, when Fitzgerald had sold a few stories, Ober wrote to him: "I am breaking my word to Max Perkins as I told him I would try to get him some money out of the next check I got for you, but I am sure he will understand the situation and agree with me that the best thing for all of us is for you to be free to work on this series [of stories for the Post]" (in Fitzgerald and Ober, 1972).

Fitzgerald never owed Perkins personally more than $3,000 at any one time, but the amount was that high on many occasions. The editor explained to a friend that he loaned the money personally because "there simply was no business justification in this house for running his debt up further. I wanted to enable him to keep at writing and avoid Hollywood and that sort of racket." In the middle of 1936, Fitzgerald pleaded his case directly to Charles Scribner, asking for $1,500. The check was sent, but Perkins and Scribner began to examine Fitzgerald's account. His total debt, not including that payment, was $6,000 (Berg, 1978).

In that same year, Fitzgerald's mother died, and he was assured the sum of $20,000 from her estate. However, the amount was held up because of legal entanglements. Perkins wrote to him:

If you are sure to get $20,000 in six months, doesn't this offer you your big chance! You have never, since the very beginning, had a time free from the necessity of earning money,—You have never been free from financial anxiety. Can't you now work out a plan to get at least eight months, or perhaps two years, free from worry by living very economically, and work as you always wanted to, on a major book? Certainly it seems to me that there is your opportunity (in Fitzgerald and Perkins, 1971).

Perkins' advice fell on deaf ears. Within a month Fitzgerald was wiring desperately:

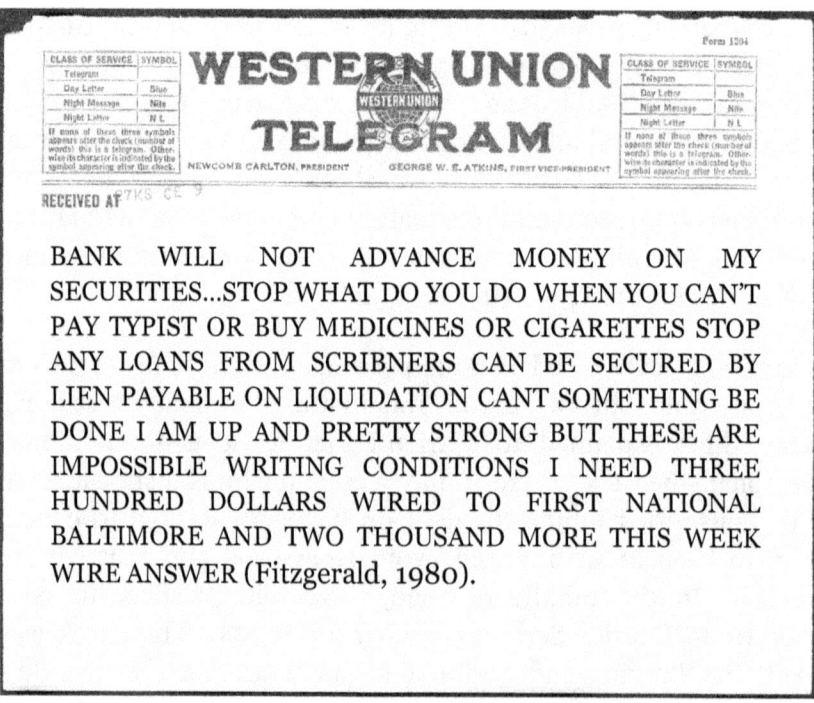

BANK WILL NOT ADVANCE MONEY ON MY SECURITIES...STOP WHAT DO YOU DO WHEN YOU CAN'T PAY TYPIST OR BUY MEDICINES OR CIGARETTES STOP ANY LOANS FROM SCRIBNERS CAN BE SECURED BY LIEN PAYABLE ON LIQUIDATION CANT SOMETHING BE DONE I AM UP AND PRETTY STRONG BUT THESE ARE IMPOSSIBLE WRITING CONDITIONS I NEED THREE HUNDRED DOLLARS WIRED TO FIRST NATIONAL BALTIMORE AND TWO THOUSAND MORE THIS WEEK WIRE ANSWER (Fitzgerald, 1980).

This loan was not made. Instead, Perkins wrote back:

We have been talking here for a long time as a result of getting your telegram. We have to have some business justification for the money we put out. With both Charlie and me there is a strong personal element in the matter, but there is none, or hardly any, with others who do not know you and who cannot understand why your account should look as it does...We greatly want to help you and always have, but you do not half help us to do it...But we should feel much better about the whole thing and about you yourself, if you could now, with the respite which this inheritance will give you, work out some plan by which you would be producing something upon which we hope to realize,—and you would too. One successful book would clear the whole slate for you all around. Couldn't you now make a regular scheme by which you would produce such a book? (Fitzgerald and Perkins, 1971).

Yet within two months, Perkins received another desperate wire.

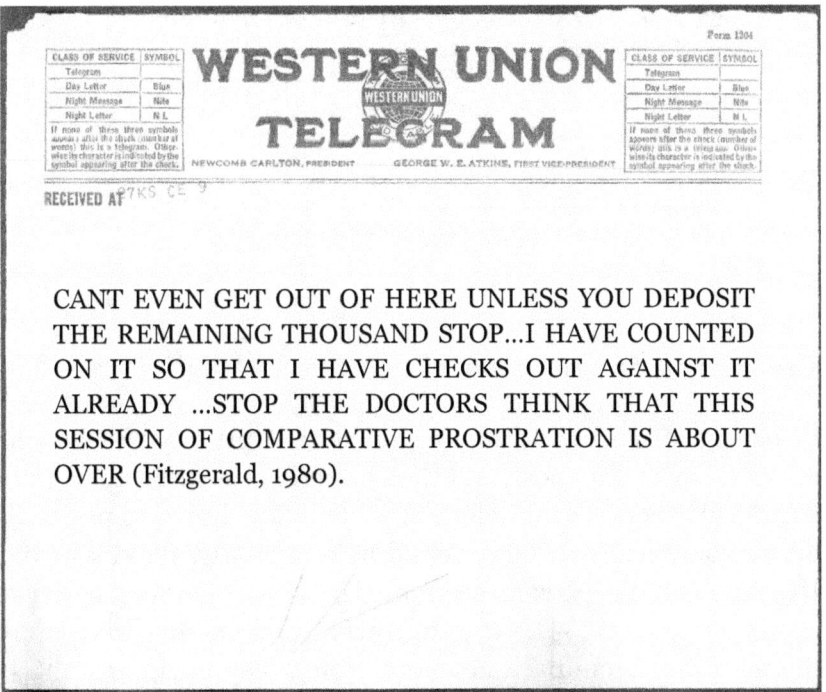

CANT EVEN GET OUT OF HERE UNLESS YOU DEPOSIT THE REMAINING THOUSAND STOP...I HAVE COUNTED ON IT SO THAT I HAVE CHECKS OUT AGAINST IT ALREADY ...STOP THE DOCTORS THINK THAT THIS SESSION OF COMPARATIVE PROSTRATION IS ABOUT OVER (Fitzgerald, 1980).

By the middle of 1937 Fitzgerald was at work in Hollywood and on the verge of finally wiping out all his debts. Before being hired by MGM his total debts were close to $40,000, including $12,500 owed personally to Ober (Fitzgerald and Ober, 1972). He instructed his agent:

> Here's the way I'd like to divide my paycheck for the moment:
>
> Per week
>
> 100   to you—commission
>
> 150   to you on debt
>
> 50   to Scribner's on debt as follows
>
> <u>first</u>, to be paid against Perkins loan
>
> <u>second</u> to be paid against insurance assignment held by Charles
>
> <u>third</u> to be paid against their movie loan on <u>Tender</u>
>
> <u>fourth</u> to be paid against my retail bill there [at the bookstore] (Fitzgerald and Ober, 1972).

This was out of a paycheck of $1,000 a week.

In paying off all his debts, Fitzgerald gave priority to Ober, to whom he owed the most, and then to Perkins as individuals over a company. Perkins told him not to be in any hurry to pay back his personal loans, but Fitzgerald paid regularly. Perkins wrote Hemingway, "My pockets are full of money from the check that comes every week. If he will only begin to dramatize himself as the man who came back now, everything may turn out rightly" (in Berg, 1978). Eventually his Scribner's debt was wiped out and Ober had to write asking what to do with the extra $50.

Fortunately, Fitzgerald did keep his sense of humor...

...about his financial situation, which is shown in his 1938 short story "Financing Finnegan," about an author constantly being bailed out by his editor:

"Only last week," said Mr. Jaggers [the editor] disconsolately, "I sent him $100. It put my department in the red every season, so I don't dare tell my partners any more. I take it out of my own pocket—give up a suit and a pair of shoes."

"You mean Finnegan's broke?"

"Broke!" He looked at me and laughed soundlessly..."You won't say anything about this, will you? The truth is Finnegan's been in a slump. He's had blow after blow in the past few years, but now he's snapping out of it and I know we'll get back every cent we've—"

He tried to think of a word, but "given him" slipped out (Fitzgerald, 1951).

In a few years, Fitzgerald turned to Ober again, and, finally, after years of an unlimited money supply, his friend and agent had to turn him down, begging his author not to start on the same treadmill again. Fitzgerald immediately wired Perkins:

> HAVE BEEN WRITING IN BED WITH TB UNDER DOCTORS NURSES CARE...OBER HAS DECIDED NOT TO BACK ME THOUGH I PAID BACK EVERY PENNY AND EIGHT THOUSAND COMMISSION. AM GOING TO WORK THURSDAY IN STUDIO AT FIFTEEN HUNDRED CAN YOU LEND ME SIX HUNDRED FOR ONE WEEK BY WIRE TO BANK AMERICAN CULVER CITY. SCOTTIE [his daughter] HOSPITALIZED WITH APPENDIX AND AM ABSOLUTELY WITHOUT FUNDS. PLEASE DO NOT ASK FOR OBERS COOPERATION (in Fitzgerald and Ober, 1972).

By Christmas 1938, the *Post* had rejected the serialization of his current novel, *Tycoon,* and he was asking again for money. When Fitzgerald finally began paying on his debt again, Perkins wrote to a friend, "I said he would do it but nobody would believe it—and sometimes I didn't either" (in Berg, 1978). His Christmas requests caused much confusion and Perkins had to write to him after the holidays: "Now these drafts are raising Cain. I think we have at last got them straightened out...But Scott, do remember that I have done all I can for the present. There was one draft more than I expected at that" (in Fitzgerald, 1980).

Later that year Fitzgerald was being hunted by a persistent creditor and protected Perkins by writing,

> Now you will notice that this letter is headed by date only. Actually I am leaving my old address and I have no new one as yet. This is an actual fact. Also I have a new agent here whose name you do not know, so if [the creditor] tries to serve a summons and complaint on me through Scribner's you can conscientiously and truly tell him that you don't know whether I'm in New Orleans or the North Pole (Fitzgerald, 1980).

At the time of his death in 1940, Fitzgerald had cleaned up many, but not all of his debts, and was working on a major novel. However, he left behind a very small estate. While it was being probated, Perkins, Ober, Murphy and the literary executor agreed upon by agent and editor arranged to loan Fitzgerald's daughter, Scottie, enough to pay her way through Vassar and give her a small allowance (Berg, 1978).

Friendship

Although the Perkins-Fitzgerald relationship was often characterized by finances, there were also strong elements of encouragement and friendship. Early in Fitzgerald's career, when some of his stories were rejected by *Scribner's* magazine, Perkins told Fitzgerald he would have no difficulty placing them in another publication, adding,

> The great beauty of them is that they are alive. 90% of the stories that appear are derived from life through the rarefying medium of literature. Yours are directly from life as it seems to me. This is true also of the language and style; it is that of the day. It is free of the conventions of the past which most writers love... [The pieces] indicate to me that you are pretty definitely lodged as a writer of short stories (in Berg, 1978).

Answering Fitzgerald's objections to publishing a collection of short stories right after *Paradise*, because he felt they would not sell, Perkins flattered him with

> They have the popular note which would be likely to make them sell in book form. I wish you did care more about writing them because of this, and also because they have great value in making you a reputation and because they are quire worthwhile in themselves (Fitzgerald and Perkins, 1971).

When the Fitzgeralds were traveling in Europe, Perkins wrote to them, "If at any time you should feel inclined to write about the things that are happening, do it because nothing would interest me more than to know of them. Moreover I should make the information into discreet but effective publicity. I have sent out a couple of notes about your trip already" (Fitzgerald and Perkins, 1971), said the editor who has been described as a terrible businessman (Perkins, 1950).

When rumors began to fly that Fitzgerald was considering switching to Boni and Liveright in 1925, he wrote to Perkins his reasons why Scribner's was his only choice as publisher:

> First. Though, as a younger man, I have not always been in sympathy with some of your publishing ideas (which were evolved under the pre-movie pre-high-literacy-rate conditions of 20 to 40 years ago), the personality of you and Mr. Scribner, the tremendous squareness, courtesy, generosity and open-mindedness I have always met there and if I may say it, the special consideration you have all had for me and my work, more than make up the difference.

> Second, you know my own idea on the advantage of one publisher who backs you and not your work and my feeling about uniform books in the matter of house and binding.

Third. The curious advantage to a rather radical writer in being published by what is now an ultra-conservative house.

Fourth. (and least need of saying) Do you think I could treat with another publisher while I have a debt, which is both actual and a matter of honor, of over $3,000? (Fitzgerald, 1963a).

In the late 1920s Fitzgerald made a brief trip to Hollywood to work and Perkins wrote him, "The trouble is that you will be so valuable to the picture people that I am afraid they will offer you almost irresistible bribes. But I have known you to resist a good deal. You always seem to know what you are about" (in Berg, 1978).

As he waited patiently, for nine years, for Fitzgerald's next novel, Perkins would write, "It is only impatience to see something one expects greatly to enjoy and admire, and wishes to see triumph. That's the truth." But as the thirties continued, so did Fitzgerald's depression and non-productivity.

In 1936 Fitzgerald gave into the entreaties of a reporter who came to interview him at a particularly low time, as he turned 40. He was bedridden with a separated shoulder, drinking heavily, and living in a hotel room in Asheville, NC, to be near Zelda's sanitarium. The interview in the New York *Post* portrayed him as a washed up symbol of the Jazz Age, and was, unfortunately, picked up by *Time* magazine. As Fitzgerald wrote to Ober,

> When that thing came it seemed about the end and I got hold of a morphine vile [sic] and swallowed four grains enough to kill a horse. It happened to be an overdose and almost before I could get to the bed I vomited the whole thing and the nurse came in and saw the empty phial and there was hell to pay for a while and afterwards I felt like a fool. And if I ever see [the writer] what will happen will

be very swift and sudden. <u>Don't tell Perkins.</u> [Underline Fitzgerald's] (Fitzgerald and Ober, 1972).

But Perkins wrote to Hemingway, "The interview he gave the *Post* was frightful. It seemed as if Scott were bent on destroying himself...I told him that [using his mother's inheritance to write a great book] was the only way to answer what the reporter had done...Well, hardly anybody reads the *Post*." He encouraged one of his other authors to visit Fitzgerald in Asheville, thanking her later, "I have known him so long, and have liked him so much, that his welfare is very much a personal matter with me, too. I would do anything to see him recover himself" (Bruccoli, 1978; Berg, 1978).

Short Story Collections and Other Works

In working with Fitzgerald on his non-novel published pieces—story collections, his play, and others—Perkins kept up the same stream of encouragement as he watched Fitzgerald's career go from success to success to failure.

The second short story collection's title, *Tales of the Jazz Age,* met with vehement opposition from the Scribner's sales staff. "There were loud and precipitous criticisms of the title...They feel there is an intense reaction against all jazz, and that the word whatever implications it actually has, will itself injure the book." Fitzgerald's reaction was to poll Zelda, two booksellers, and some friends, all of whom voted for the title. "It will be bought by my own personal public," he objected, "that is, by the countless flappers and college kids who think I am a sort of oracle." The title stayed (Berg, 1978).

As authors have always done, Fitzgerald complained about the lack of advertising of his first book of stories. Perkins wrote to him,

I think we did more advertising, very probably, than you were aware of, but it was not as effective or as plainly visible as it should have been. But we have now a man with excellent experience whom we believe will do the work with skill and vigor...I only want to ask you always to criticize freely—I am afraid you disliked writing this letter—and to convince you that, in the case of *The Beautiful and Damned,* we will work the scheme out with you so that...you will feel satisfaction both with the copy and the campaign (Fitzgerald and Perkins 1971).

At the time Perkins was urging Fitzgerald to give up the flapper, whom he had created and nurtured through her maturity. "We ought to...get away altogether from the flapper idea in advertising *The Beautiful and Damned.*" Soon after this, Fitzgerald's short story heroines began to grow up, as did the author and his wife (Berg, 1978).

The title of Fitzgerald's next collection, *All The Sad Young Men,* met with great approval, better than his original idea, *Dear Money* (Berg, 1978). In the mid-twenties, as the ideas for *Gatsby* were taking hold in his mind, Fitzgerald heard from his editor about a story he had published in *Mercury,* "Absolution," which turned out to be about the early years of his Gatsby hero:

It seemed to me very good indeed, and so different from what you had done before—it showed a more steady and complete mastery...Greater maturity might be the word. At any rate, it gave me a more distinct sense of what you could do, possibly because I have not read any of your other stories in the magazines... This seemed to show a remarkable strength and resource (Perkins, 1950).

During the year preceding publication of *Gatsby,* Perkins heard little from his author except for requests for funds. Perkins wrote to encourage him on the *Young Men* short story collection: "Two of the stories have more breadth than those of earlier collections.

In fact, it is remarkable that you have been able to make them so entertaining for the crowd when they have so much significance...Those who have believed in you can now utter another decisive 'I told you so'" (in Berg, 1978).

Zelda wrote a novel as part of her therapy, published by Scribner's as *Save Me the Waltz* in 1932, and Perkins was in the position of referee as well as editor. Zelda had sent her book directly to Perkins without letting Fitzgerald see it. She defended her action to her husband by saying, "I know Max will not want it and I prefer to do the corrections after having his opinion" (in Fitzgerald and Perkins, 1971; Fitzgerald, 1980).

Fitzgerald was worried about Hemingway's reaction, cautioning Perkins:

> Ernest told me once he would "never publish a book in the same season with me," meaning it would lead to ill-feeling. I advise you, if he is in New York (and always granting you like Zelda's book), do not praise it, or even talk about it to him!...There is no possible conflict between the books but there has always been a subtle struggle between Ernest and Zelda, and any apposition might have curiously grave consequences —curious, that is, to un-jealous men like you and me (Fitzgerald, 1963a).

During the dry period after *Tender*, Fitzgerald at one time began work on a medieval novel, parts of which were serialized in *Redbook,* encouraged by Perkins. Publishing it, said his editor, "would do what we want by publishing a book by you and keeping you on the map—You may think you are more off it than you are, for when you do a book it will have attention." Fitzgerald never finished this novel (Berg, 1978; Fitzgerald and Perkins, 1971).

MANAGER AS MUSE 87

In his period of despair, Fitzgerald wrote a series of articles for *Esquire*, published as "The Crack Up." Many, including Hemingway, saw these as final proof that Fitzgerald was washed up. But Perkins' eternal belief in his author helped him to rationalize his feelings about the series to Hemingway:

> Nobody would write those articles if they were really true. I doubt if a hopeless man will tell about it...Those people I should think would not say anything at all, just as those who really intend suicide never tell anybody. So I thought that in some deep way, when he wrote those articles, Scott must have been thinking that things would be different with him (in Berg, 1978).

Both Perkins and Ober felt that these articles damaged Fitzgerald's career and urged him to stop writing them (Bruccoli, 1978). After Fitzgerald's death, Edmund Wilson decided to bring out a group of Fitzgerald's *Esquire* pieces under the title *The Crack Up*. Perkins did not like the idea and would not publish the volume. The book, as published by New Directions, became a "catalyst for the Fitzgerald revival," says Bruccoli (1978).

Involvement in Their Personal Lives

As friend as well as editor to Fitzgerald, Perkins inevitably became somewhat involved in his personal life, especially his drinking habits. One of Perkins' friends said later, "Scott sobered up and tried to put on a show when Max came to Baltimore, and to this day I don't know if Max actually saw through him, but those efforts kept Scott going and Max accepted them as though they were genuine—perhaps they were, perhaps Max reached the truth in him as he did in everyone." She realized later that Perkins had been wise to Fitzgerald all along (Berg, 1978).

In the 1940s when Fitzgerald was in Hollywood drinking with the stars, Perkins impishly drew a picture of him at the end of one of his letters with a glass of Coke in his hand. Fitzgerald took offense at the implication, and Perkins had to defend his joke.

"There was nothing implied by that drawing. I thought you would admire the art.—and the man was not meant to be you. It was meant to be me, and to indicate my own good resolutions. Don't read any hidden meanings into what I write or draw" (in Bruccoli, 1978; Fitzgerald, 1980).

The editor's forays into Fitzgerald's personal life even included arranging for a rug to be removed from his Great Neck home. "I'm in rather a predicament," Fitzgerald wrote from Europe. "My other friends there are drunk and unreliable [so] I'm going to ask you [to take care of it]....but I don't know what else to do as everybody in Great Neck is either incapable or crooked" (Fitzgerald, 1980; Berg, 1978).

At the end of Fitzgerald's life, Perkins (1950) wrote him with great encouragement,

> As for your position, it is a mighty high one. I never see an editor or writer, hardly, but they ask about you. It shows what you did, for think of all the writers who were thought to be notable, and whose output has been much larger, who have simply vanished without a trace. But we know that *Gatsby* was a truly great book...You know that you are in almost all the school anthologies.

In one of his last letters to Perkins, Fitzgerald mused on his own immortality,

> I wish I was in print. It will be odd a year or so from now when Scottie assures her friends I was an author and finds that no book is procurable. It is certainly no fault of yours. You...have been a friend through every dark time in these five years (Fitzgerald, 1963b).

Originally Fitzgerald had named Ober as his literary executor, but after their argument, he crossed out his name and wrote in Perkins' in pencil. The legality of this was in question after his death. Eventually both men renounced their claim in favor of

Judge John Biggs, an old Princeton friend of Fitzgerald's. However, Perkins was the one called on to make every decision regarding the author's literary legacy (Berg, 1978).

This Side of Paradise and *The Beautiful and Damned*

Fitzgerald's first draft of a novel, *The Romantic Egotist,* was written when he was a young lieutenant stationed stateside during the First World War. He sent it to a friend from Princeton who passed it on to his own publisher, Scribner's (Berg, 1978). Fitzgerald received an unsigned letter from the publisher which was almost certainly written by his future editor:

Dear Sir:

> We have been reading *The Romantic Egotist* with a very unusual degree of interest;—in fact no manuscript novel has come to us for a long time that seemed to display so much originality...We generally avoid criticism as beyond our function...but we should like to risk some very general comments this time because, if they seemed to you so far in point that you applied them to a revision of the manuscript, we should welcome a chance to reconsider its publication...

> We do not want anything we have said to make you think we failed to get your idea in the book,—we certainly do not wish you to "conventionalize" it by any means in either form or manner, but only to do those things which it seems to us important to intensify its effect and so satisfy a reader that he will recommend it,—which is the great thing to accomplish toward a success...We hope we shall see it again and we shall then reread it immediately (in Fitzgerald, 1980).

Reading the revision, Perkins was thrilled to find his hunch was correct. He found an ally in Old CS's son, Charles III, but the older editors voted the book down (Berg, 1978).

Determined to see it published, Perkins actually sent the book to two rival publishers. Both turned it down, to Perkins' relief. A fellow Scribner's editor remembered that Perkins was "terrified that they would accept it, for all the time he saw how vitally it might still be improved" (in Berg, 1978).

When the editor and author first met, one of the suggestions Perkins gave Fitzgerald was to change the narrative from the first to the third person. The final version that arrived on Perkins desk in September of 1919 had all his changes incorporated and a new title: *This Side of Paradise* (Berg, 1978).

The manuscript was circulated among those on the editorial board, who appeared to be eager to argue against the book. Old CS went first, saying, "I'm proud of my imprint. I cannot publish fiction that is without literary value." Brownell pronounced it frivolous. Old CS then said to Perkins, "Max, you're very silent" (in Berg, 1978). As Berg describes the scene:

> Perkins stood and began to pace the room. "My feeling," he explained, is that a publisher's first allegiance is to talent and if we aren't going to publish a talent like this, it is a very serious thing." He contended that the ambitious Fitzgerald would be able to find another publisher for this novel and young authors would follow him: "Then we might as well go out of business...If we're going to turn down the likes of Fitzgerald, I will lose all interest in publishing books." The vote of hands was taken. The young editors tied the old. There was a silence. Then Scribner said he wanted more time to think it over.

Perkins' practical argument was what impressed CS enough to change his mind. The book was accepted (Lynn, 1978).

The editor wrote to his new author excitedly, using the editorial "we":

> I am very glad, personally, to be able to write to you that we are all for publishing your book...I was afraid that when we declined the first manuscript, you might be done with us conservatives. I am glad you are not. The book is so different that it is hard to prophesy how it will sell, but we are all for taking a chance and supporting it with vigor (Perkins, 1950).

As the publication date drew near, all of Scribner's began to pick up Perkins's enthusiasm. Cowley said later that even before publication the book was known as "the terrifying voice of a new age, and it made some of the older employees of Scribner's cringe" (in Berg, 1978). A week after it exploded onto the lists, Scott Fitzgerald and Zelda Sayre were married, his fortune assured, so they thought.

Perkins and Fitzgerald, both terrible spellers, began noticing all the misprints their haste had let creep into the book. Perkins took the blame. "He had been so frightened of the reaction to the book from the other employees," Berg (1978) explains, "that he had hardly let it out of his hands during any stage of its preparation —not even to proofreaders." All the misspellings, however, became as much a conversation topic as the book itself. The renowned columnist FPA (Franklin P. Adams) of the New York <u>Tribune</u> turned the search for errors into a parlor game. Fitzgerald was very upset when many of the errors on FPA's list were uncorrected even in the sixth printing (Berg, 1978).

But with the success of *Paradise,* Perkins was vindicated and looking forward to his star author's second book.

Fitzgerald's second novel was similar to his first, although lacking the excitement of *Paradise.* Perkins did not need to work closely with Fitzgerald on revisions, but was more concerned with getting his young literary star through the second novel which many promising writers falter on. As they got to know each other better, Fitzgerald began to speak his mind rather than blindly follow his editor's advice.

Fitzgerald completed his draft of *The Beautiful and Damned* at the end of April 1921. He delivered the manuscript in person and asked for $600 to pay for a pair of steamship tickets to Europe (Berg, 1978).

Perkins wrote to Fitzgerald, "The galleys are demoralizing the stenographers on the fourth floor, I mean as to work. I even saw one taking some proofs out to lunch with her...because she could not stop reading it. That is the way with all of them who are near enough to get their hands on the proofs—not only the stenographers" (in Berg, 1978).

At the end of the year, Fitzgerald and Perkins had one of their first disagreements. The editor asked the author to tone down one of his character's speeches concerning the Bible. Fitzgerald wrote to Perkins, "If it was an incident which I felt had no particular literary merit I should defer to your judgment without question but that passage belongs beautifully to that scene and is exactly what was needed" (Fitzgerald and Perkins, 1971).

Perkins' response is typical of the way he would always work with his authors to keep their integrity and that of their writing:

> Don't ever defer to my judgment. You won't on any vital point, I know and I should be ashamed if it were possible to have made you, for a writer of any account must speak solely for himself...
>
> My point is that you impair the effectiveness of the passage —of the very purpose you use it for—...and I wish you would try so to revise it so as not to antagonize even the very people who agree with the substance of it. You would go a long way toward this if you cut out "God Almighty" and put "Deity." In fact, if you will change it on

the line indicated, by that change you will have excised the element to which I object.

I hope this gets over to you. If I saw you for 10 minutes I know you would understand and would agree with me (Perkins, 1950).

Fitzgerald took his editor's advice.

A month after publication, Perkins wrote to Fitzgerald,

> [*The Beautiful and Damned*] is going on at about the same pace it held when you were here. It has sold about 33,000 copies actually. I doubt if we can hope that it will be an overwhelming success now, but when you speak of me as being disappointed, you're wrong. I think that the book has consolidated your position...,—has convinced people that...*This Side of Paradise* was very far indeed from being all (Fitzgerald and Perkins, 1971).

The Great Gatsby

Fitzgerald's classic represents the high point of his career, as well as Perkins influence. Besides his encouragement to get his author to write a more significant and substantive book than he had in the past, Perkins had a great effect on the text itself. Some of his tentative suggestions were taken by Fitzgerald and turned into the most memorable parts of the novel.

Fitzgerald's own feelings about his talents changed while he was working on *Gatsby*. He realized his weaknesses and approached it with a firmer hand and a more formal sense of structure (Hoffman, 1951). Eble (1964), who analyzed the actual drafts and revisions Fitzgerald made on the manuscript, said:

> An admirer of Fitzgerald—of good writing, for that matter—reads the draft with a constant sense of personal involvement, a sense of small satisfied longing as the right word gets fixed in place, a feeling of strain when the draft version hasn't yet found its perfection of phrase, and a nagging sense throughout of how precariously the writer dangles between the almost and the attained. "All good writing," Fitzgerald wrote his daughter, "is <u>swimming under water</u> and holding your breath"...Throughout the pencil draft, Fitzgerald made numerous revisions which bring out his chief traits as a reviser: He seldom threw anything good away, and he fussed endlessly at getting the right things in the right places.

By April of 1924 he had started and stopped a dozen times, and Perkins was concerned but tactful. In preparing the fall list, he told Fitzgerald he wanted his name on it, which was enough motivation to get the author working again. He wrote to Perkins, "While I have every hope and plan of finishing my novel in June, you know how those things often come out. And even [if] it takes me ten times that long I cannot let it go out unless it has the very best I'm capable of in it or even as I feel sometimes, something better than I'm capable of" (in Berg, 1978; Fitzgerald and Perkins, 1971).

Perkins replied with his usual encouragement:

> So far as we are concerned, you are to go ahead just at your own pace, and if you should finish the book when you think you will, you will have performed a very considerable feat even in the matter of time...
>
> If we had a title which was likely ...we could prepare a cover and a wrap and hold them in readiness for use. In that way, we would gain several weeks if we should find that we were to have the book this fall... The last thing we

want to do is to divert you to any degree, from your actual writing, and if you let matters rest just as they are now, we shall be perfectly satisfied. The book is the thing and all the rest is inconsiderable beside it (Fitzgerald and Perkins, 1971).

Among Fitzgerald's first titles was *Among the Ash Heaps and Millionaires,* which Perkins did not like. "I do like the idea you have tried to express," Perkins explained, "the weakness is in the words 'Ash Heap' which do not seem to me to be a sufficiently definite and concrete expression of that point of the idea…I always thought that *The Great Gatsby* was a suggestive and effective title." Although Perkins had not seen the manuscript and had little knowledge of the content, this was among the titles Fitzgerald had tossed out casually early on (in Berg, 1978).

Perkins' push to get a dust jacket designed actually lead to one of the most effective symbols in the book. The early jacket drawing showed two enormous eyes—presumeably Daisy's—brooding over an amusement park version of New York City. In August of 1924, Fitzgerald wrote Perkins: "For Christ's sake, don't give anyone that jacket you're saving for me. I've written it into the book," as the omniscient brooding billboard of Dr. TJ Eckleburg, whose large eyes look down on the action (Mizener, 1974).

Fitzgerald sent the manuscript off before he was totally satisfied with it. "Do tell me the absolute truth, <u>your first impression of the book,</u> and tell me anything that bothers you in it" (in Berg, 1978). His editor read it in one sitting, and cabled immediately, "THINK NOVEL SPLENDID," writing the next day:

> I think the novel is a wonder. I'm taking it home to read again and shall then write my impressions in full; but it has vitality to an extraordinary degree and <u>glamour</u>...It has a kind of mystic atmosphere at times that you infused into <u>Paradise</u> and have not since used...And as for sheer writing, it is astonishing (in Berg, 1978).

In his later detailed criticisms Perkins wrote,

> It is an extraordinary book, suggestive of all sorts of thoughts and moods...I have only two actual criticisms.

> One is that among a set of characters marvelously palpable and vital—I would know Tom Buchanan if I met him on the street and would avoid him—Gatsby is somewhat vague. The reader's eyes can never quite focus upon him, his outlines are dim...Couldn't he be physically described as distinctly as the others, and couldn't you add one or two characteristics like the use of that phrase "old sport"—not verbal but physical ones, perhaps. I think that...a reader—this was true of Mr. Scribner and of [Perkins' wife]—gets an idea that Gatsby is a much older man than he is...But this would be avoided if on his first appearance he was seen as vividly as Daisy and Tom are, for instance—and I do not think your scheme would be impaired...

> The other point is also about Gatsby: His career must remain mysterious, of course...It did occur to me, though, that you might here and there interpolate some phrases, and possibly incidents, little touches of various kinds, that would suggest that he was in some active way

mysteriously engaged. You do have him called on the phone, but couldn't he be seen once or twice consulting at his parties with people of some sort of mysterious significance, from the political, the gambling, the sporting world, or whatever it may be. I know I am floundering, but that fact may help you to see what I mean...I wish you were here so I could talk about it to you, for then I know I could at least make you understand what I mean...

The general brilliant quality of the book makes me ashamed to make even these criticisms. The amount of meaning you get into a sentence, the dimensions and intensity of the impression make a paragraph carry, are most extraordinary. The manuscript is full of phrases which make a scene blaze with life...

You once told me you were not a <u>natural</u> writer—My God! You have plainly mastered the craft, of course; but you needed far more than craftsmanship for this (Perkins, 1950).

Fitzgerald replied enthusiastically, "Your wire and your letters made me feel like a million dollars." He agreed with all Perkins' criticisms. He also asked for several hundred dollars more, bringing his advance on the book to an even $5,000, and a lower royalty percentage on this book, as his way of paying interest to Scribner's on his loans. Eventually they compromised at 15% of the retail price of $2 on the first 40,000 copies and 20% thereafter (Berg, 1978).

To his editor's suggestions, Fitzgerald replied,

Your criticisms are excellent and most helpful, and you picked out all my favorite spots in the book to praise as high spots. Except you didn't mention my favorite of all— the chapter where Gatsby and Daisy meet...<u>I myself didn't know what Gatsby looked like or was engaged in</u>

and you felt it. If I'd known and kept it from you you'd have been <u>too impressed with my knowledge to protest.</u> This is a complicated idea but I'm sure you'll understand (in Berg, 1978).

Later, he expanded on Perkins' idea: "After having had Zelda draw pictures until her fingers ache I know Gatsby better than I know my own child. My first instinct after your letter was to let him go and have Tom Buchanan dominate the book...but Gatsby sticks in my heart. I had him for a while then lost him and now I know I have him again" (in Berg, 1978).

The other editors were still not crazy about Perkins' brash young author. But when reading *Gatsby,* the old codger himself WC Brownell, came out of his office one day and called to the other staff members, "May I read you something beautiful?" reciting two full pages from <u>Gatsby</u> (in Berg, 1978).

As publication drew closer, Fitzgerald's confidence faltered, especially about the title. He wired in early March asking to change it to *Gold-Hatted Gatsby*. Perkins wired back that the delay would be harmful and would cause much confusion. Throughout his life, Fitzgerald felt the title was always the book's fatal flaw. Perkins received another cable from his author on Capri: "CRAZY ABOUT TITLE UNDER THE RED WHITE AND BLUE. WHAT WOULD DELAY BE?" Perkins told him it would be several weeks, wiring "THINK IRONY IS FAR MORE EFFECTIVE UNDER LESS LEADING TITLE. EVERYONE LIKES PRESENT TITLE URGE WE KEEP IT." Three days later, another wire appeared: "YOU'RE RIGHT" (in Berg, 1978).

An entire week passed before Perkins had any news to report and then he had to cable, "SALES SITUATION DOUBTFUL. EXCELLENT REVIEWS," which was actually more optimistic than warranted on both counts (Berg, 1978).

Two weeks later he wired, "DEVELOPMENTS FAVORABLE REVIEWS EXCELLENT," writing later, "One thing...we can be sure of: That when the tumult and shouting of the rabble of reviewers and gossipers dies, *The Great Gatsby* will stand out as a very extraordinary book" (Fitzgerald and Perkins, 1971).

Perkins also had to tell Fitzgerald of rumors that he was thinking of switching to Boni and Liveright, and he asked Fitzgerald for any details he knew. "LIVERIGHT RUMOR ABSURD," he wired. It depressed Fitzgerald that Perkins would ever believe such a story and he wrote,

> Now Max, I have told you many times that you are my publisher, and permanently, as far as one can fling about the word in this too mutable world. If you like I will sign a contract with you immediately for my next three books. The idea of leaving you has never for <u>one single moment</u> entered my head (in Berg, 1978).

Later, during Fitzgerald's depressing Hollywood years, Perkins reminded him, "What a pleasure it was to publish [*Gatsby*]! It was as perfect a book as I ever had a share in publishing. One does not...get such satisfactions as that any more" (Madison, 1966).

A few months before he died, Fitzgerald implored Perkins to bring out *Gatsby* again:

> Would the 25c press keep *Gatsby* in the public eye—or <u>is the book unpopular:</u> Has it had its chance?... But to die, so completely and unjustly after having given so much! Even now there is little published in American fiction that doesn't slightly bear my stamp—in a <u>small way</u> I was an original...I have not lost faith. People will <u>buy</u> my new book...
>
> Love to all of you, of all generations.
>
> Scott (Fitzgerald, 1963b)

Tender Is the Night and *The Last Tycoon*

Perkins and Fitzgerald had their longest stretch of work together on *Tender*. Perkins had to keep up his stream of encouragement for nine years, without pushing Fitzgerald too hard lest he give up. During this time, Fitzgerald had to work at other more lucrative pursuits—stories—to finance treatment of his wife's worsening illness and his own physical and mental problems.

Perkins wrote to him about the money situation in July after *Gatsby's* publication,

> If [some deposits of money] puts you in a position to go straight ahead with a new novel, we are certainly mighty glad to send it. A new novel is what you ought to do as soon as you are able...If you could give me some idea of what you are doing in it, just in the briefest way, I wish you would;—but merely as a matter of interest, and not at all if you think that talking about it in advance is dangerous, I know it does sometimes dull the edge for the writer to do this (Fitzgerald and Perkins, 1971).

Fitzgerald continued to promise a June deadline as late as April 1927, believing he would get an extended burst of work and finish it up. He asked for and received a $6,000 advance that year. Perkins knew, however, that what he really needed was a quiet place to work and suggested Wilmington, Delaware (Bruccoli, 1963; Turnbull, 1962). In March of 1927 the Fitzgerald family settled there, where they lived until leaving for Europe two years later.

The sale of rights to a play and movie based on *Gatsby* kept Fitzgerald going for a year or two. He wrote for the *Saturday Evening Post* at $3,500 per story, neglecting his novel, which he was receiving advances on. At the start of 1928, Fitzgerald wrote Perkins, "Patience yet a little while. I beseech thee and thanks eternally for the deposits," telling his "banker" that he could be written off as a "safe investment and not as a risk," since he was on the wagon since October and smoking only Sanos, a popular non-nicotine cigarette (in Berg, 1978).

Perkins replied, "I think we ought all to be proud of the way you climbed on the water wagon. It is enormously harder for a man who has no office hours and has control of his own time,—and it is hard enough for anybody." But Perkins was concerned about the lengthening time since the publication of *Gatsby* (Berg, 1978).

By June Fitzgerald was writing friends from France, "Two more chapters finished. All completed August," and writing to Ober in that month, "Novel nearly finished." But the manuscript shows no reason for this optimism (Berg, 1978).

Perkins reported to a mutual friend later that year that "Scott has not finished his novel, and I have only had one letter from him...In that he mentioned it as if he did not like to talk about it, and I get very bad reports of him...Couldn't you write him a letter? Letters are not much help but one from you would help him more than one from anyone else" (Lardner and Perkins, 1973).

Over in Paris, James Joyce was visiting the Fitzgeralds for dinner and commented that *Finnegans Wake,* on which he had been working for six years, was coming along. "Yes, I expect to finish my novel in three or four years more at the latest," he crowed. Fitzgerald was encouraged, noting to Perkins, "He works 11 hours a day to my intermittent eight" (in Berg, 1978).

Fitzgerald tried to economize by living in cheaper hotels, but to no avail. Early in 1930 he asked for $500 to cover his Christmas bills. To Perkins' subtle questioning he replied, "To begin with, because I don't mention my novel isn't because it isn't finishing up or that I'm neglecting it—but only that I'm weary of setting dates for it till the moment when it is in the post office box!" (in Berg, 1978).

In March of that year, Perkins wrote again,

> Ober yesterday gave me reason to hope that a large part of your novel would be here before long. I'll tell you when we get that into our hands, and a publication date set, we'll let loose everything we have got in the way of salesmanship and advertising...There is no author who commands a more complete loyalty than you do (Fitzgerald and Perkins, 1971).

Two years later he was still working, and writing to Perkins, "I am re-planning [the novel] to include what's good in what I have...Don't tell Ernest or anyone—let them think what they want." The Hemingway critic hanging over his shoulder was one of Fitzgerald's greatest motivations to get things done (in Mizener, 1974).

Eight years after the publication of *Gatsby,* with no Fitzgerald novel on the list, Perkins now came up with a plan to eliminate Fitzgerald's debt by having the new novel serialized. That did the trick. By September of 1932, Fitzgerald was promising a complete draft by the end of the month. "I will appear in person carrying the manuscript and wearing a spiked helmet. <u>Please do not have a band as I do not care for music</u>." He appeared before a much surprised Perkins right on schedule with the first section of what was to be *Tender Is the Night*. Perkins pronounced it "wonderfully good and new" (Berg, 1978).

Cosmopolitan stepped in with an offer of serialization and Perkins pushed hard for final revisions, causing Fitzgerald to work dangerously close to the magazine's deadline (Mizener, 1974). Perkins always felt that his suggestion to serialize was what finally got Fitzgerald to finish *Tender*. "Authors must eat and magazines must live," he explained. "He had to do it once that was agreed upon" (Berg, 1978).

Fitzgerald still needed money, but Scribner's couldn't possibly offer any more advances. Perkins came up with the idea of providing a $2,000 loan, at 5%, to be repaid on the sale of the movie rights. Perkins' hopes at this time were higher than his author's (Berg, 1978).

The book is dedicated to Sara and Gerald Murphy, Fitzgerald's models for his main characters, writing to Perkins, "My only regret is that the dedication isn't to you, as it should be, because Christ knows you've stuck with me on the thing through thick and thin, and it was pretty thin going for a while" (Fitzgerald, 1980).

Perkins was not fond of the title, *Tender Is the Night*, but he was sure of the quality of the writing. Wheelock remembers Fitzgerald waiting for the office to open in the morning so anxious was he to revise the galleys. Wheelock maintains that, despite his drinking, Fitzgerald's judgment was unimpaired, and claims he was the only author he had ever known who could revise reliably while "obviously tight" (Turnbull, 1962; Fitzgerald, 1980).

In April 1934 the book was finally published with a first printing of 7,600 copies. There were two more small printings, and then it died after 15,000 copies. It did not recover the money Fitzgerald had been advanced against it (Bruccoli, 1978).

Hollywood gave Fitzgerald plenty of material to work with for his next and final novel, *The Last Tycoon*. His hero was modeled after young studio head Irving Thalberg. During his difficult Hollywood years, after the first rush of work and a regular paycheck, only Perkins, his secretary, and Graham stood by him, remembering. "We knew how painfully he was dredging up the prose-poetry in *The Last Tycoon* from the depths of his being" (Graham, 1976).

Only months after *Tender* was out, Fitzgerald was asking for money and Perkins was giving it, but this time with reservations: "We deposited the hundred, but you know, Scott, it is not quite the same here as in the old days when we had a dictatorship" (Fitzgerald and Perkins, 1971).

Two years later, when his financial situation had not improved, Scribner wrote to him,

> Therefore, after deducting the unearned balance on *Tender* ..., there is a deficit in your account of $5,818.09, not taking into account the $1,500.00 which you have just assigned on your life insurance policies...
>
> All this is rather painful and I hope it will not give you a headache. Max and I thought it only fair, however, by you as well as ourselves to get the figure on paper, to make sure that we agreed with you (Fitzgerald, 1980).

But *Collier's* magazine rejected the serialization of *Tycoon*, and Graham reports that Fitzgerald said to her sadly, "They wanted to see more. They wanted to be sure that I was capable of finishing the novel." The next day, however, Fitzgerald received a wire from Perkins stating,

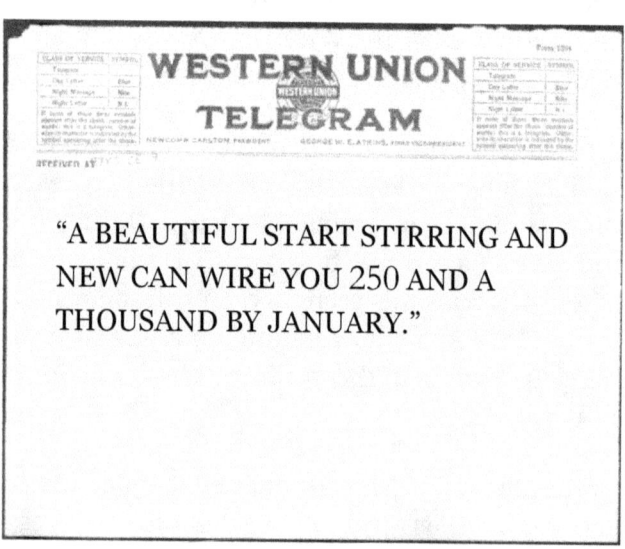

"A BEAUTIFUL START STIRRING AND NEW CAN WIRE YOU 250 AND A THOUSAND BY JANUARY."

This was a personal loan from Perkins, and not a Scribner's advance (Fitzgerald, 1980; Graham, 1976). Perkins followed up with the usual encouraging letter: "I thought the book had the magic that you can put into things" (Fitzgerald and Perkins, 1971).

The following month Perkins was writing to him again, "I think what you have done is most excellent...I am not interested in it only for Scribner's or even only for you, but because I want to see what you have in you, justify itself.—So any time you have a chance to tell me how things go on, do it as briefly as you please" (Fitzgerald and Perkins, 1971).

However, soon after Fitzgerald's death that December, Perkins wrote to a friend, "This book which might have vindicated him—for the first part of it was extremely promising—was far from finished" (in Berg, 1978).

Perkins tried to salvage the unfinished novel, briefly considering having Hemingway complete it. But Zelda wisely insisted that the idea be dropped. Finally, Edmund Wilson was chosen as editor and the book was published in 1941, unfinished, with notes, *The Great Gatsby*, and a selection of stories (Bruccoli, 1978).

Perkins tried at the same time to revive interest in Fitzgerald generally. He heard rumors that Princeton had begun to look with disfavor upon their almost-alumni. To end the rumors he tried to persuade them to bring out a book in Fitzgerald's honor, but to no avail (Berg, 1978).

After Fitzgerald's death, Perkins wrote to Graham about *Tycoon*, "The first chapter alone is good enough to stand by itself. It breaks a man's heart to see what this book could have been" (in Graham, 1976).

Ernest Hemingway

Ernest Hemingway was born in Oak Park, Illinois, in 1899 to a middle-class family. He and his older sister were raised as twins, and, perhaps to escape his doting mother, he joined the Italian Red Cross during World War I as an ambulance driver and returned home a decorated hero. He worked as a cub reporter for the Kansas City *Star*, lived in Chicago, married his first wife, Hadley Richardson, and made friends with established novelist Sherwood Anderson. He was able to go abroad as a foreign correspondent for the Toronto *Star*, and, with a letter of introduction from Anderson, found himself in the best place for a writer to be, Paris in the 1920s. He quickly became a protégé of Gertrude Stein and Anderson, and, after drafting a first novel, wrote a bitter parody of Anderson's style.

Word of the young writer traveled so fast in Paris literary circles that Fitzgerald recommended him to Perkins sight unseen or unread in 1925, and Perkins, along with Anderson's publisher, Boni and Liveright, pursued him. Scribner's won because Boni and Liveright did not dare to publish the parody of their best author, and Hemingway insisted that this be published before his promising first novel, *The Sun Also Rises*. Scribner's agreed to the terms, and Perkins fought, once again, for acceptance by the Scribner's editors.

Aside from refereeing fights (on at least one occasion, physically), stroking egos and watching sales increase, Perkins did little for Hemingway in the way of editing copy. Neither did anyone else. His output under Perkins peaked with *For Whom the Bell Tolls* (1940), which hit the bestseller list and was sold to the movies for a large sum.

Hemingway's Major Works
Hemingway's publishing career began when Contact Press, run by Robert McAlmon in Paris, brought out *Three Stories and Ten Poems* (1923), and then *in our time* (1925), a collection of short stories. This was reprinted in the US as *In Our Time* by Boni and Liveright (1925).
His next novels were edited by Perkins and published by Scribner's:
The Torrents of Spring (1926)
The Sun Also Rises (1926)
A Farewell to Arms (1929)
For Whom the Bell Tolls (1940)
As well as collections of short stories, essays, and non-fiction
Men Without Women (1927)
Death in the Afternoon (1932)
Winner Take Nothing (1933)
The Green Hills of Africa (1935)
To Have and Have Not (1937)
The Fifth Column and the First Forty-Nine Stories (1938)

Scribner's published two of Hemingway's novels after Perkins' death:
Across the River and Into the Trees (1950)
The Old Man and the Sea (1952)
And posthumously:
A Moveable Feast (1964), non-fiction
By-Line: Ernest Hemingway (1967), journalism
Islands in the Stream (1970), novel
The Dangerous Summer (1985), non-fiction
The Garden of Eden (1986), novel
True at First Light (1999), novel, and
Under Kilimanjaro (2005), non-fiction

Perkins accompanied Hemingway on fishing trips in Key West, somewhat in awe of his macho author. Hemingway always had a deep respect and affection for his editor, and never turned against him as he did with many other friends from his early days. After Perkins' death in 1947, Hemingway remained with Scribner's, and dedicated his novella, *The Old Man and the Sea,* to his late editor. Hemingway's work after this is considered to be slight at best, and he committed suicide, like his father and sister before him, and his brother and granddaughter after him, in July of 1961 with a shotgun blast to his head (Baker, 1969; Berg, 1978; Hemingway, 1962; Plimpton, 1974).

Hemingway's publishing relationship with Scribner's was affected by Fitzgerald's career and personality from the start. One of the main differences between the two was their attitude toward money. Novelist Nelson Algren said that Hemingway "never went for the money. He made the money, he liked the money, he spent the money. But he never went for the money" (Berg, 1978).

Hemingway's beginnings as a war correspondent greatly influences his style; he practiced saving words by using cable-ese. At this time he was more than willing to learn as much as he could from great writers such as Stein, Anderson and Ezra Pound, who copy edited his early efforts as no future editor would dare (Cunliffe, 1964). Of this early work, Stein told him, "There is a great deal of description in this, and not particularly good description. Begin over again and concentrate." As Stein described her early mentoring sessions in *The Autobiography of Alice B. Toklas* (1933):

> One day she [Stein] said to [Hemingway] Look here, you say you and your wife have a little money between you. Is it enough to live on if you live quietly? Yes, he said. Well, she said, then do it. If you keep on doing newspaper work, you will never see things, you will only see words and that will not do—that is of course if you intend to be a writer. Hemingway said he undoubtedly intended to be a writer.

From other writers he learned the difference between plain reporting and real writing. Pound took out his adjectives; Stein developed his simplicity of expression. He also gained a feeling for point of view and the power of description (Hoffman, 1955).

Although Fitzgerald acted as a pseudo-agent for Hemingway, he, like other friends and influential people, did little editing of his writing. Fitzgerald explained to O'Hara:

> The only effect I ever had on Ernest was to get him in a receptive mood and say let's cut everything that goes before this. The pieces got mislaid and he could never find the part that I said to cut out. And so he published it without that and later we agreed that it was a very wise cut. This is not literally true and I don't want it established as part of the Hemingway legend, but it's just

about as far as one writer can go in helping another (in Bruccoli, 1978).

After the immense success of *Sun* in 1926, whose rights he assigned to Hadley upon their divorce, he began work on a second novel and a second wife, heiress Pauline Pfeiffer. The success of *A Farewell to Arms* helped Hemingway financially but not nearly as much as Pauline's inheritance did, paying for African safaris, a house in Key West (bought for $8,000) with a staff of five servants, and numerous hunting and fishing trips. He wrote no novels during this time, however, until the novella *To Have and Have Not* in 1937, a critical and financial failure. Although the thirties were a bad time for his novels, he did produce two of his best short stories in this period, "The Short Happy Life of Frances Macomber" and "The Snows of Kilimanjaro" (Donaldson, 1977).

The Depression did not affect his career or popularity. The former war hero reveled in his new-found legendary status. Although he could name his price for short stories, he agreed to do stories for the fledgling magazine *Esquire* for a mere $300 a piece because he enjoyed writing them (Donaldson, 1977).

Upon his divorce from Pauline when he was 40, Hemingway had to depend on his own financial resources, but he had plenty to depend on by that time. However, he still asked Perkins for a $1000 advance on his new novel, and Pauline helped him to pay his taxes the first year after they were divorced (Donaldson, 1977).

Later in his career, Liveright tried to persuade Hemingway back into their fold with a guaranteed advance of $3,000 on any novel, $1,000 on any book of short stories or essays, and straight 15% royalties from the beginning. Hemingway was not to be tempted. Liveright also offered to buy the rights to *Torrents* and *Sun* and reissue them in uniform editions with *In Our Time*. He told Liveright's emissary that he was "absolutely satisfied" with Scribner's (Baker, 1969).

After a tour of duty in the Spanish Civil War, Hemingway married a third wife, correspondent Martha Gellhorn, and wrote a third novel, *For Whom the Bell Tolls*. An enormous financial success, this work marked the peak of Hemingway's career under Perkins' editorship, although his legendary status grew throughout his lifetime and beyond.

Work Habits

Hemingway had a new wife for each major novel: Hadley for *Sun*, Pauline for *Arms*, Martha for *Bell*, and Mary for *The Old Man and the Sea* and all the rest of the works. Only Martha was also a writer and, in fact, one of Perkins' best authors. Even Hemingway gave her credit: "Marty is writing beautifully. I know so much more about the trade than she does and can help her in so many ways. She has great talent and what she needs is a good editor" (Hemingway, 1976).

Like many writers, Hemingway thought of his craft as a trade that he was continually learning and at the mercy of. He told his son Gregory of his own try at writing, "Writing's got to flow and come easy if it's good and this stuff 'smells of the lamp.' You know that old phrase—smells like you've been up all night working on it over a kerosene lamp" (James, 1957; Hemingway, 1976; Hemingway, 1962)

In another letter he described his feelings in the most Hemingway-esque phrase possible: "I love to write and I love to write well" (Cousins, 1976).

In the 1950s, Hemingway was among many writers interviewed by George Plimpton (1974) for a series of articles on "Writers at Work" for the *Partisan Review*:

[GP]: How about financial security? Can that be a detriment to good writing?

[EH]: If it came early enough and you loved life as much as you loved your work it would take much character to resist the temptations. Once writing has become your major vice and greatest pleasure only death can stop it. Financial security then is a great help as it keeps you from worrying. Worry destroys the ability to write. Ill health is bad in the ratio that it produces worry which attacks your subconscious and destroys your reserves... You can write any time people will leave you alone and not interrupt you. Or rather you can if you will be ruthless enough about it...

[GP]: What would you consider the best intellectual training for the would-be writer?

[EH]: Let's say that he should go out and hang himself because he finds that writing well is impossibly difficult. Then he should be cut down without mercy and forced by his own self to write as well as he can for the rest of his life. At least he will have the story of the hanging to commence with...For a long time now I have tried simply to write the best I can. Sometimes I have good luck and write better than I can.

Living in Cuba, when his status required him to lead a more social life, he would take guests into Havana for a meal at a cafe, but shunned nightclubs. He would come home early if he had tough writing to do the next day. Nothing would keep him from his job (James, 1957).

When talking to other people for information, Hemingway did not take notes, but relied on his memory. He usually wrote his drafts in longhand because the typewriter made it seem too easy and "the product looked so solidified in type that he hesitated to make any changes by way of improvement," according to

Donaldson (1977). In his later years, he would write stories on the typewriter, but the first drafts of *Islands in the Stream* were in longhand. He would not dictate because "It leads to rhetorical excesses that did not untangle well on the page," explains Donaldson (1977).

Wherever he lived, Hemingway had a special space for writing, often in his bedroom, sometimes on a very large, flat top desk. At other times he wrote standing up at a bookcase, chest high in the midst of clutter, leaving just enough room for a typewriter. He had a reading board on top of the typewriter and wrote on one sheet of onionskin paper at a time on the board, in pencil. His handwriting over the years became larger, more childish, with little punctuation and few capital letters. He used the typewriter only when the writing was going fast (*Newsweek*, 1958).

When Hemingway had one of his many bad accidents, which left him with a broken arm making it almost impossible to write, his wife, Pauline, offered to take down *Death in the Afternoon* by dictation. But he felt that anything that was to be read by the eye must be written by the hand and, in the words of Baker (1969), "checked by the ear and the eye in the process."

His work schedule during most of his professional life was to wake at about 6:30 a.m. without the help of an alarm clock. Hemingway claimed he had exceptionally thin eyelids which made him extra sensitive to sun, causing him to wake at first light. By 8 a.m. he would be at work. With passages of description or exposition, the writing went slowly. But pages of dialogue would come rapidly. "When the people are talking," he said, "I can hardly write it fast enough" (in James, 1957).

To start, he would re-read what he had written the day before and would then take up where he had left off. He did not use an outline or structured plan. He would quit at about noon when there was still some juice left and would do other things to keep the writing off his mind so he could return to the work refreshed the next morning (Donaldson, 1977).

Hemingway usually averaged four hours a day at his desk, but sometimes went for as long as six. Like Wolfe, he would count his daily wordage, ranging from a low of 200 to a high of 1,000. "The best time to stop," he said, "is when you are going good and when you know what will happen next. If you do that every day when you are writing a novel, you will never get stuck" (in James, 1957).

Looking back on his earlier years, Hemingway said,

> I was trying to write then and I found the greatest difficulty, aside from knowing truly what you really felt, rather than what you were supposed to feel, and had been thought to feel, was to put down what really happened in action. [I was trying to put down] the actual things which produced the emotion that you experienced (in Cowley, 1954).

Hemingway, like Fitzgerald, was his own copy editor and ruthless when attacking the text.

> The test of a book is how much good stuff you can throw away...I use the oldest words in the English language when I write. People think I'm an ignorant bastard who doesn't know the $10 words. I know the $10 words. There are older, better words, and if you arrange them in the proper combination, they stick (in Baker, 1961).

He would throw away anything that did not ring true, anything that sounded rhetorical or overdone. Baker (1961) claims that the reason his writing went so slowly was because of the high standards he held himself to, wanting everything to be perfect in the first draft so it would require no revision. "He talked a lot about revising, but he did very little," Baker said. However, at the time of Hemingway's death, Baker reported that a completed manuscript —*A Moveable Feast*—was at his publisher but was not considered finished because he had not "worked it through line by line and often word by word" (James, 1957; Smith, 1969).

For whatever qualities inherent in Perkins' or Hemingway's character, his editor was one of the few people he never became alienated from, never rebelled against, never rejected. Perhaps this was because Perkins never asserted his claim on him, never tried to control Hemingway, but quietly directed his enormous talent as best he could and kept the writer writing.

Relationship with Perkins

[GP]: What about the influence of some...people—your contemporaries—on your work? What was Gertrude Stein's contribution, if any? Or Ezra Pound? Or Maxwell Perkins?

[EH]:...This backyard literary gossip while washing out the dirty clothes of 35 years ago is disgusting to me...Here it is simpler and better to thank Gertrude for everything I learned from her about the abstract relationship of words, say how fond I was of her, reaffirm my loyalty to Ezra as a great poet and a loyal friend, and say that I cared so much for Max Perkins that I have never been able to accept that he is dead. He never asked me to change anything I wrote—except to remove certain words which were not then publishable. Blanks were left, and anyone who knew the words would know what they were. For me he was not an editor. He was a wise friend and a wonderful companion. I liked the way he wore his hat and the strange way his lips moved (Plimpton, 1974).

Although Perkins had little to do with the actual text of Hemingway's novels, the editor was an influence on his work and life in many other ways.

Hemingway expected many special services from those around him, especially his publishers. He left his fly fishing rods with

Perkins and when one of the tips got broken there was an enormous uproar. Hemingway blamed the company for criminal negligence and threatened to leave. At that time, they were also storing his shotgun shells in their printing plant. Scribner worried that if they had caused the building to blow up, he would have blamed the company for that, too (Scribner, 1977).

Hemingway's brother Leicester reports that when Charles Scribner was coming to pay a visit to Key West, the writer became unusually sociable. "For this occasion, he got a haircut, wore a necktie, and ordered the champagne iced in advance. Ernest was very ingenuous about the responsibility of a writer to his publisher. 'Mind you, I wouldn't give an unprintable for all the others, but Charlie is the exception,' he explained. And he ordered me to get a haircut too" (Hemingway, 1962).

At the time Fitzgerald brought Hemingway to Scribner's attention, he was unpublished but being wooed by other publishers. He chose Perkins, not the company, on the basis of Fitzgerald's recommendation and the letters the editor had written him. They showed "a sympathy, an interest, and a capacity for critical discernment which suggested that the firm of Scribner's would be a proper place to do business," in Baker's words (1956).

Perkins' help was invaluable in the beginning of Hemingway's career, but the editor felt he needed even more assistance later, "because he wrote as daringly as he lived." Perkins believed that Hemingway's writing displayed the grace under pressure characteristic of his heroes, and that he was prone to overcorrect his own copy. "He once told me that he had written parts of...*Arms* 50 times," Perkins said. "Before an author destroys the natural quality of his writing—that's when an editor has to step in. But not a moment sooner" (in Bruccoli, 1978; Berg, 1978).

Perkins realized early in their relationship how sensitive his tough author was. When *Scribner's* magazine accepted

Hemingway's story "Fifty Grand" on the condition that he would shorten it, Perkins wrote to Fitzgerald, "I wish with his very first story that we did not have to bring this up [because Hemingway] is one of those whose interest is much more in production than in publication, and he may revolt at the idea of being asked to conform to an artificial specification in length." In fact, he would not cut the story, and the *Atlantic Monthly* printed it, making Perkins fear Scribner's would lose their new author (Berg, 1978).

To get him working during a dry period after *Sun*, Perkins wrote asking him to put together a collection of his stories, promising, "Your [new] book will be among those most prominently presented by us." This excited Hemingway, who wrote back right away with a tentative title and a list of stories. This made Perkins even more eager and they got to work right away on the collection (in Berg, 1978; Baker, 1969).

The following year, Hemingway's father shot himself, and he confided in Perkins that his father was the parent he really cared about. Berg (1978) notes that from that time on, he felt closer to his editor. "Max became the solid, trustworthy older man in Hemingway's turbulent life, someone to turn to and rely on."

Later, lying in a hospital bed with a broken arm and unable to write, he suggested to his publisher that he could make more money by insuring him. "Since signing on with Perkins, he had suffered an anthrax infection, a cut in his right eyeball, a forehead gash from a skylight, congestion of the kidney, a sliced index finger, a torn chin, a branch run through his leg, and now a break in his chief professional tool, the right arm," as Baker (1969) said.

When rumors inevitably surfaced that he was restless and wanted to change publishers, Hemingway assured Perkins that he had no intention of doing so. He wanted Scribner's to be the publisher of his collected works and offered to put his feelings in writing. Perkins was reassured, as the rumors had bothered him.

"One night in a nervous moment, when the rumors were flying thick and fast, I wrote you by hand asking you if you would be willing to write a letter saying they were foundless. But then in the end, I tore up my letter because I thought it was only part of the game and that we should take our own medicine" (in Berg, 1978).

Perkins proved his own loyalty to his author by passing up a chance to sign on William Faulkner in 1930. Wheelock felt that Perkins was "afraid of arousing Hemingway's jealousy...In Hemingway's mind, there was no more room in Max's life for another power so threatening as William Faulkner. Hemingway's was a mighty ego, and Max knew it" (in Berg, 1978).

Hemingway was also jealous of the time Perkins spent with Wolfe. In 1934 he told his editor that his pet writer's stories were "pretentious." After Wolfe left Scribner's, Hemingway assured Perkins that he was not impressed with the way Wolfe had portrayed his editor in his novel. He boasted that he could get Perkins straighter in 1,000 words than Wolfe had in 10,000 (Baker, 1969).

When Hemingway went to Spain in 1938, he wrote Perkins a long letter aboard ship apologizing for being "trying" recently. He thanked his editor for his loyalty through his bad tantrums and "general shittiness." Despite his premonitions of mortality, Hemingway assured Perkins that "writing is a hard business," but that nothing made him feel better (in Berg, 1978).

The letter sounded funereal and worried Perkins about his writer's general state of mind. He wrote back assuring Hemingway that no thanks were necessary: "I think you have treated us swell. We all do. I owe you plenty." Perkins wrote to Fitzgerald about his problems trying to help Hemingway, "I wish I could talk to you about him: He asked me about a plan he has, and I advised him quite vigorously, and yet had some doubts of the wisdom of it afterward. But I think it is right enough. I only would like to talk to someone who really would understand the thing" (Fitzgerald and Perkins, 1971).

Hemingway did quite well financially during his lifetime. In 1941 his earnings were $137,357, and he had saved $85,000 in a special account. However, he felt that this would not be enough for all his expenses and applied to Scribner's for a personal loan of $15,000. About this same time Hemingway was involved in a plagiarism suit which was thrown out of court. However, the $1,000 bill for legal fees was debited against his royalties, which did not please him. He complained that Charles Scribner should know better than to "cut steaks out of his racehorses, adding that he would rather commit hara kiri than submit to further robbery. Next day, typically, he cabled an apology. Charlie must disregard his angry night letter," as Baker (1969) describes the exchange.

Hemingway's son Gregory cites Perkins' "unwavering decency" as the reason for Hemingway's continued loyalty to his editor even during what Berg (1978) calls his "blossoming megalomania" of the late thirties. Hemingway once promised to stay with Scribner's if Perkins agreed never to fight with him "because you are my most trusted friend as well as my God damned publisher." He pleaded with him to realize that his current dry period was not because he had "become a rummy or a problem writer," but that he wanted to write so much that sometimes it was "worse than being in jail not to have the time to do it." For the past year, 1942, he literally had not had one hour to put words to paper. But he was gathering information all the time, and he would be able to create out of this material. Perkins never even hinted to Hemingway that he did not believe him, but he did confide to a colleague, "I'm afraid Ernest's believing his own legends about himself...and that he might never be able to write truly again" (in Berg, 1978).

Perkins told a young would-be writer of an incident that had happened earlier with Hemingway in Key West.

> I went to visit Ernest Hemingway, after he had been a couple of years in Key West. We went fishing every day in those many-colored waters and then also in the deep-blue Gulf Stream. It was all completely new to me, and wonderfully interesting...I said to Hemingway, "Why don't you write about all this?" and he said, "I will in time, but I couldn't do it yet," and, seeing I did not get his meaning, he pointed to a pelican that was clumsily flapping along, and said, "See that pelican? I don't know yet what his part is in the scheme of things." He did know factually in his head, but he meant that it all had to become so deeply familiar that you knew it emotionally as if by instinct, and that that only came after a long time, and through long unconscious reflection (Perkins, 1950).

As Hemingway's editor, Perkins' main duties were to "listen to his braggadocio prating and to cushion criticism when it came," in Epstein's (1978) words. Epstein also points out that two of Hemingway's worst books, *The Green Hills* and *To Have* were produced under Perkins, and it is not clear whether Perkins knew they were weak. He sums up, "The moral would seem to be that the best of editors cannot prevent the worst of books."

If Perkins' biggest defense of Fitzgerald was in the field of finance, with Hemingway it was in the area of those infamous four letter words. He got Hemingway to tone them down by writing, "The majority of people are more affected by words than things...I think some words should be avoided so that we shall not divert people from the quality of this book to the discussion of an utterly unpertinent and extrinsic matter" (in Berg, 1978).

When Perkins died, Scribner wrote to tell Hemingway, ending with "I never had a better friend." Hemingway cabled sympathy and in a follow up letter called his editor one of his best and most loyal friends, and wisest counselors in life as well as writing. Hemingway mused that nothing could bother Perkins now, and he would not have to worry any more about being the executor of Wolfe's "chickenshit estate," or keep women writers from building nests in his hat (Baker, 1969).

Non-Fiction Works and Short Stories

When Fitzgerald was not writing, he assuaged his guilt feelings by recommending other young authors to his publisher. In early October of 1924, Fitzgerald wrote his editor about a young American living in Paris who wrote for the *transatlantic review* saying, "He has a brilliant future. Ezra Pound published a collection of his short pieces in Paris at some place like the Egotist Press. I haven't it hear [sic] now but it's remarkable and I'd look him up right away. He's the real thing." Fitzgerald misspelled his name—as he always would—"Hemmingway." Perkins sent to Paris to get copies of the books (in Berg, 1978).

Perkins was surprised by the sound of the new and distinctive writing from this young find. He wrote to him,

> I was greatly impressed by the power in the scenes and incidents pictured, and by the effectiveness of their relationship to each other...I doubt if we could have seen a way to the publication of this book *[in our time]* itself on account of material considerations: It is so small that it would give the book sellers no opportunity for substantial profit if issued at a price which custom would dictate. This is a pity, because your method is obviously one which enables you to express what you have to say in very small compass (in Berg, 1978).

This first letter to Hemingway was lost because of an incorrect address. When Perkins got the right address he sent a second letter, including a carbon copy of the first to show his enthusiasm. Hemingway was at this time writing and skiing in Austria. Before he had a chance to call for his mail, he received a cable from Anderson's publishers, Boni and Liveright, offering an advance of $200 on publishing the *in our time* stories and a request for immediate acceptance by cable. Hemingway agreed (Baker, 1956).

Liveright published the stories as *In Our Time*, with an option to have the first look at his next effort. Now Scribner's and other publishers, particularly Harcourt, were also interested. Critics have felt that Hemingway wrote his next work, *The Torrents of Spring*, a vivid satire on Liveright's star author, Anderson, to give Liveright something to turn down, freeing him from his contract. He wrote to Fitzgerald at this time, "Am turning down a sure thing for delay and a chance but feel no regret because of the impression I have formed of Maxwell Perkins through his letters and what you have told me of him. Also confidence in Scribner's and would like to be lined up with you" (in Bruccoli, 1978).

Fitzgerald entered the fray by cabling Perkins in early January 1926,

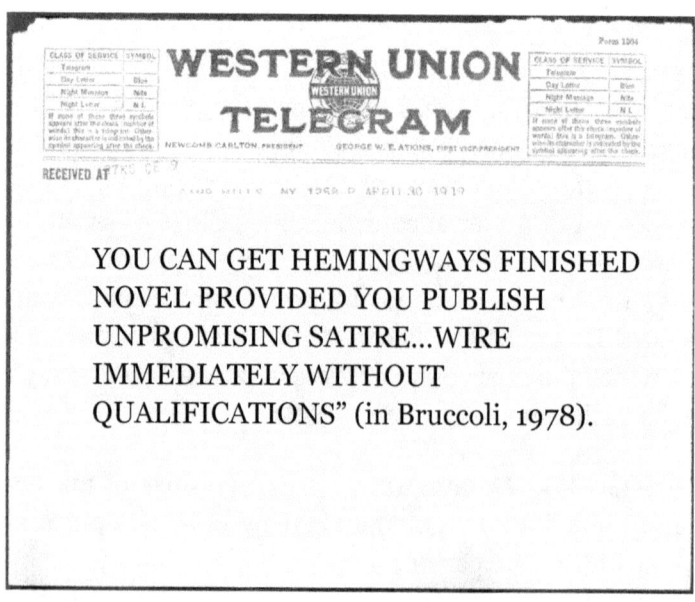

YOU CAN GET HEMINGWAYS FINISHED NOVEL PROVIDED YOU PUBLISH UNPROMISING SATIRE...WIRE IMMEDIATELY WITHOUT QUALIFICATIONS" (in Bruccoli, 1978).

Perkins did so:

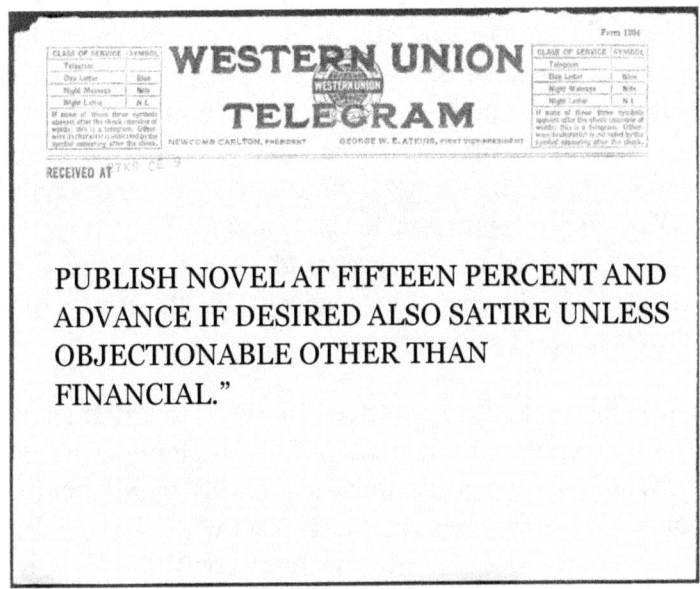

"PUBLISH NOVEL AT FIFTEEN PERCENT AND ADVANCE IF DESIRED ALSO SATIRE UNLESS OBJECTIONABLE OTHER THAN FINANCIAL."

A few days later he cabled again:

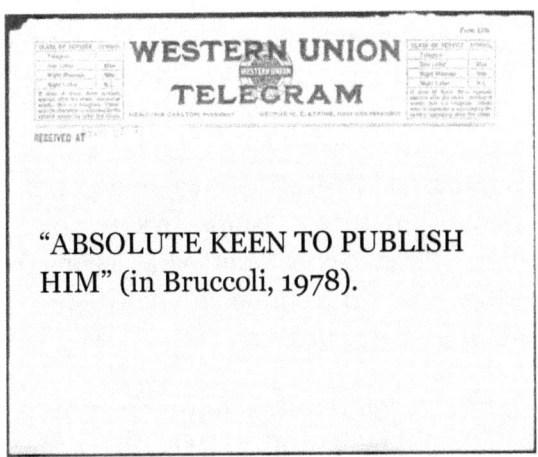

"ABSOLUTE KEEN TO PUBLISH HIM" (in Bruccoli, 1978).

Perkins followed up his cables with a letter to Fitzgerald:

> I believe as compared with most others [publishers], Hemingway would be better off in our hands because we are absolutely true to our authors and support them loyally in the face of losses for a long time, when we believe in their qualities and in them. It is that kind of a publisher that Hemingway probably needs, because I hardly think he could come into a large public immediately...He ought to be published by one who believes in him and is prepared to lose money for a period in enlarging his market (in Bruccoli, 1978; Fitzgerald and Perkins, 1971).

Once Liveright officially rejected *Torrents,* word traveled fast. Knopf and Harcourt both made offers to Hemingway. But the young writer had given his word to Perkins months before that he would get first crack at his novel, with the condition of publication of the satire thrown in (Berg, 1978).

Hemingway arrived in New York from Paris in February of 1926. Perkins offered a $1500 advance on the satire and the novel, against a 15% royalty. These terms may have been standard in the industry, but not for an unknown writer's parody and first novel. Perkins was buying Hemingway, and, given the future return, it proved to be a shrewd investment (Baker, 1969; Bruccoli, 1978).

Torrents was published in May of 1926, and Perkins reported to Fitzgerald that it received "some praise but not always comprehension." Perkins' own personal feeling was that the humor in the book kept it from being totally "devastating" to its target, Anderson (in Berg, 1978).

Hemingway's first major non-fiction work was his explanation of his love of bullfighting, *Death in the Afternoon.* One of his loudest tirades against Scribner's came at this time. The galleys he received had a slug head on each one: "Hemingway's Death." To a man who was, in Donaldson's (1977) words, "convinced that language had a power to jinx a man," it was very upsetting, and he let them know it.

The book was published in September of 1932 and sales began well. Perkins' first reports to Hemingway were encouraging. The most biting criticism of all came from Max Eastman who wrote a review entitled "Bull in the Afternoon" which enraged Hemingway. Perkins did his best to cool the situation by saying that it did not amount to anything. "The reality is in the quality of what you write," Perkins told him, "and cannot be hurt by anyone" (Baker, 1969; Berg, 1978). Months later, when Hemingway ran into Eastman in Perkins' office, they got into a legendary fistfight which ended with Perkins pulling the critic off the writer.

Perkins tried immediately to distract his author with a new short story collection. Hemingway took up the gauntlet and got to work writing some "pretty good" stories and picking the pieces he wanted to include in *Men Without Women*. He chose 14 for Perkins to arrange, a task which Perkins took very seriously. His tendency was to put the strongest pieces in the beginning, middle and end, and alternate different stories of varying quality back to back in the rest of the book (Berg, 1978).

Hemingway's next major work was non-fiction, *The Green Hills of Africa*. Perkins was excited about the idea from the first, writing, "Couldn't you modify the title (which I am altogether for, in general) to 'In the Highlands of Africa'? It would imply something that happened, or things that happened there. Without the "In" as a title alone, it might be what they call a 'travel' book" (Perkins, 1950).

Upon getting the proofs back in late August 1935, Perkins felt everything was in order except for Hemingway's backhanded swipe at his mentor, Stein. Perkins wrote Hemingway that "I think it was better not to call the old girl a bitch." Hemingway pointed out that he had not mentioned her by name and no one could prove it was she. He also wondered what could be used in place of bitch? He would gladly modify it with "les" or "lesbian," but bitch certainly fit Stein. He did not see what all the fuss was about unless Perkins was just worried that it would give the critics something else to "burp about." Eventually Hemingway conceded and changed the reference to "female." He figured that would make her the most angry and keep Perkins happy (Berg, 1978).

In January of the next year Hemingway wired his editor that he had finished with his Gulf Stream novel, *To Have and Have Not*. Perkins was excited because he felt the book had one great "superficial advantage in being about a region that I think nobody has ever written well about, and a very rich and colorful scene." He remembered eight years earlier when Hemingway had told him that he could not write about the waters until he understood even the pelican's role. "But you did get around to it when you had absorbed a sense of it and knew what part everything did play in the scheme of things" (in Berg, 1978).

Hemingway had his doubts about it. It was too short, and he wanted to add some short stories. His idea was for a "living omnibus," with the overall title *To Have and Have Not*, including his 50,000 word novella, "Harry Morgan." That way Scribner's could promote it as a major work and the buyer would get his or her money's worth. Perkins would, of course, have to assemble all this because, in Berg's (1978) paraphrase of Hemingway's letter, "There was going to be a lot of blood spilled in Spain during the next several months and Hemingway wanted to be there, ringside." He promised to deliver the manuscript by July 1937.

When *To Have* was published in mid-October of that year, Hemingway was in Madrid, but followed the sales figures closely and worriedly. He cabled Perkins three times in a little over a month just to find out how it was going. By early November, it was fourth among the national best sellers, with 25,000 copies sold. The reviews, however, were, at best, "mixed" (Baker, 1969).

Perkins did not say much more to Hemingway about his own disappointment over the writing of the Harry Morgan stories. He once told his daughter, "When you have a suggestion for Ernest you have to catch him at the right time." Perkins knew that Hemingway wanted unquestioned support, not even constructive criticism (Berg, 1978).

In the most public Fitzgerald-Hemingway fight with Perkins as referee—Hemingway's jab at Fitzgerald in "The Snows of Kilimanjaro"—Perkins was indeed the player holding the trump card. He had been there when the original remark was made. The only ones present were Hemingway, Perkins and writer Molly Colum, not Fitzgerald. Hemingway had said portentously, "I am getting to know the rich." Colum did him one better by saying, "The only difference between the rich and other people is that they have more money." To be topped, and by a woman no less, was more than Hemingway's ego could stand, and he made the witty remark his own and gave the victim's comment to Fitzgerald in the story (Berg, 1978):

> He remembered poor Scott Fitzgerald and his romantic awe of [the rich] and how he had started a story once that began, "The very rich are different from you and me." And how someone had said to Scott, Yes they have more money. But that was not humorous to Scott. He thought they were a special glamorous race and when he found they weren't it wrecked him just as much as any other thing that wrecked him (in Berg, 1978).

Perkins looked down on this episode, a feeling which he expressed to others but not to Hemingway. He wrote to Fitzgerald, "As for what Ernest did, I resented it, and when it comes to book publication I shall have it out with him. It is odd about it too because I was present when that reference was made to the rich, and the retort given, and you were many miles away." He wrote later to assure Fitzgerald that the reference would be cut. "As for Ernest, I know he will cut that page out of his story. He spoke to me a while ago about it, and his feelings toward you are different from what you seem to suspect. I think he had some queer notion that he would give you a 'jolt' and that it might be good for you, or something like that. Anyhow, he means to take it out" (Berg, 1978; Bruccoli, 1978).

When Perkins was working on the next collection of stories with Hemingway, he wrote to Fitzgerald saying that he wished he could talk to him about Hemingway. He also told him about the new collection. "One of the new stories is 'The Snows of Kilimanjaro,' and you are not in it" (Bruccoli, 1978).

He later reminded Hemingway about his promise, "And by the way you were going to take out F. Scott Fitzgerald, weren't you, from 'The Snows of Kilimanjaro'?" He changed the passage but kept the name "Scott," requiring Perkins to respond,

> You amended it very neatly.—But I greatly wish his name could come out altogether. If people reading the story do not identify "Scott" as F. S. F., it might as well be some other name (one realizes he is a writer in the very next sentence) and if they do identify him, it seems to me it takes them out of the story for a moment. It takes their attention to the question of what this means about Scott. You did take out the things that could hurt and I showed the amended passage to two people...and they thought Scott might still feel badly, being very sensitive, but that they hardly thought there was much reason for it now. If his name could come out without hurting it would be good—But I'll bring up the matter when you are here (in Bruccoli, 1978).

On publication, the name was changed to "Julian" (Berg, 1978).

While planning *Bell,* Hemingway told Perkins about some stories he wanted to write. The one he had the most worked out was about an old fisherman alone fighting a swordfish for days and nights and winning, only to have the sharks finish it out because he could not boat it. When he published this novella, *The Old Man and the Sea,* Hemingway honored his late editor by dedicating it to him (Berg, 1978). As Baker (1969) tells the story,

> Sitting by the pool in the heavy heat of May 30th, 1952, [Hemingway] decided that *[The Old Man and The Sea]* would be dedicated "To Mary and to Pilar his boat." But it was Memorial Day and he began to think of friends who had died. That evening he told Mary that he wanted to inscribe the book "To Charlie Scribner and to Maxwell Perkins." She magnanimously agreed.

The Sun Also Rises

> When I was 25, I read novels by Somersault Maugham and Stephen St. Vixen Benet. They had written novels and I was ashamed because I had not written any novels. So I wrote *The Sun* when I was 27, and I wrote it in six weeks, starting on my birthday, July 21st, in Valencia, and finished it September sixth, in Paris. But it was really lousy and the rewriting took nearly five months (Hemingway in Ross, 1962).

Like most Hemingway anecdotes, this does have some truth in it. He did complete the first draft in that time period in 1925, and reworked it in the winter. In March he finished it, and had it typed professionally, and in May sent it to Perkins (Baker, 1956; Baker, 1979).

Hemingway was with his wife and son on the French Riviera in early June when he reluctantly showed the first draft to Fitzgerald. In his usual manner, Fitzgerald gave his young friend a "long and frank" critique. He condemned the "carelessness, ineffectuality, wordiness, condescending casualness," in Baker's

(1979) words, and the "sheers, superiorities, and nose-thumbings-at-nothing," in Fitzgerald's words, in the opening chapters. "You've done a lot of writing that honestly reminded me of Michael Arlen," thrown in as a pointed jab at Hemingway. As Baker (1979) notes, "Nothing could have been more shrewdly calculated to turn Hemingway's stomach than Fitzgerald's comparison, particularly because Arlen's heroine...bore at least some resemblance to...[*Sun*'s] Brett Ashley." However, Fitzgerald's insult got him to work. In June of 1926 Hemingway wrote Perkins that he had thrown out the first 15 pages because they had nothing in them that was not explained later.

As Fitzgerald basked in the Riviera sun, and Perkins was in New York reading the bad first draft, Hemingway was in Paris, drenched in the continual rain. Perkins' letter was just what he needed:

> [*Sun*] seems to me a most extraordinary performance. No one could conceive of a book with more life in it...The book is an "astonishing" [work of art] the more so because it involved such an extraordinary range of experience and emotion, all brought together in the most skillful manner—the subtle ways of which are beautifully concealed—to form a complete design. I could not express my admiration too strongly (in Berg, 1978).

As Scribner's worked on the book, rumors began to fly in publishing circles that the rest of the company was not as enthusiastic as Perkins. The editor was worried enough to bring the manuscript home and discuss it with his wife, feeling that it was not just the words but also the subject itself that was shocking. With a clenched fist she told her husband, "You've got to stand up and fight for it, Max" (in Berg, 1978).

As to the "dirty word" problem, Perkins wrote Hemingway:

> The book is of course a healthy book...But as I have said, people are afraid of words. We don't want to divert

attention from its intrinsic qualities to details of purely extrinsic importance. It would be a pretty thing if the very significance of so original a book should be disregarded because of the howls of a lot of cheap, prurient moronic yappers. You probably don't appreciate this disgusting possibility because you've been too long abroad, and out of that atmosphere. Those who breathe its stagnant vapors now attack a book, not only on grounds of eroticism which would not hold here, but upon that of "decency," meaning words (in Berg, 1978).

At the monthly board of editors meeting, when Charles Scribner was 72 and still very much in charge, he indicated that *The Sun* had indeed stunned him. He was wise enough, however, to seek the advice of a friend, a Boston judge who was a contemporary of Scribner's and also a novelist. The judge was, of course, appalled by the language, but admired the novel. "You must publish the book, Charles. But I hope the young man will live to regret it" (in Berg, 1978).

The inevitable debate over the novel raged at the editorial meeting. Perkins argued that a larger question than just the book was at stake. He later wrote to the younger Scribner, who was not at the meeting, that the question was "a crucial one in respect to younger writers—that we suffered by being called 'ultra conservative' (even if unjustly and with malice) and that this would become our reputation for the present when our declination of this book should, as it would, get about." He defended the language vigorously. "But if they belong, if they are the words that would actually be used in the circumstances of the book, then artistically they should be used and an author feels as if he's playing false in evading them," he explained (in Berg, 1978; Madison, 1966).

Old CS listened once again to Perkins' presentation, as he had for *This Side of Paradise* seven years earlier, slowly shaking his head from side to side. A junior editor at the time who heard gossip about the meeting, told Cowley in confidence, "Perkins was the new idea and the younger people in the place were terrifically for him. I remember the moment of crisis...We knew that Perkins had to go to bat for Hemingway, and it was reported with hushed voices one evening that Charles Scribner, Jr. had turned down the book and Perkins was going to resign" (in Berg, 1978).

When the vote was over, Perkins walked back to his office and wrote to a friend, "We took it with misgivings," admitting that his view "influenced our decision largely...I simply thought in the end that the balance was slightly in favor of acceptance for all the worry and general misery involved" (in Berg, 1978).

From this first novel on, Perkins was unusually hesitant to offer advice to Hemingway. For one thing, as Berg (1978) says, the book was different "in style and subject from any book Maxwell Perkins had ever edited—or even read." Fitzgerald cautioned Perkins about his new author, "Do ask him for the absolute minimum of necessary changes, Max— he's discouraged about the previous reception of his work by publishers and magazine editors (though he loved your letters)" (Fitzgerald, 1963a).

After publication, the epigraph from Ecclesiastes still bothered Hemingway. He wanted to cut the words "vanity of vanities, saith the preacher" to emphasize his "real point" that the "earth abideth forever." Perkins agreed. This theme, said the editor, "has not been remarked upon by most reviewers, but I often doubt if the emotion itself...is felt by...people of the book-reading class. I believe it is felt by simpler people" (Berg, 1978).

As expected, Scribner's mail was filled with irate reaction to *The Sun*. The book was banned in Boston and disgusted readers across the country demanded an apology from Scribner's. Perkins became an expert at answering these letters as he was still getting protests about that "foul-mouthed, vulgar, blustering upstart" Fitzgerald (in Berg, 1978).

The Sun proved, however, to be a tremendous critical and financial success. As Burlingame (1946) mused in retrospect, "Its sale convinced editors like Max Perkins that another generation, 'lost' though it might be, had found an understanding of the writing craft of which most of their elders had little enough."

As the sales grew, Perkins wrote to Hemingway, "*The Sun* has risen...and is rising steadily." Eventually the sale reached 20,000 copies and years later, when Hemingway was being wooed by other publishers, he credited the high sales totals to Scribner's vigorous advertising support. Berg (1978) notes that Hemingway did not know how much personal support Perkins had given the book as well.

In the hubbub that followed publication, Perkins wrote to Fitzgerald:

> Somehow rumors very damaging to us have got about that Ernest is dissatisfied with his publisher. He knew about this before we did, and wrote me that there was nothing in it whatever, but there is nothing that can be done to stop it, and every other house is perfectly willing to pass it on, and to take the excuse for going to Ernest with an offer...One publisher rushing to him who, when *The Sun*...appeared said of Scribner's:—"A great publisher sunk to the gutter," and another publisher sends over a delegation whose younger men read aloud passages from *The Sun* in derision, at a director's meeting. You would think they would be too ashamed of their original position to do this (Fitzgerald and Perkins, 1971).

A Farewell to Arms

In Paris in 1927 Hemingway was on a daily six-hour writing regimen for his second novel. In a month he wrote 30,000 words and announced his decision to move back home after four years overseas. He confessed to Perkins that he had "busted up" his personal life, and that at least his editor had helped him keep his professional life balanced. He told Perkins that he had started the novel, but did not give much detail, due to his consistent feeling that, in Berg's (1978) words, "the more books were talked about the slower they progressed."

Hemingway revised the manuscript first in pencil, then with a typewriter, for six hours every day. His sister typed each day's batch of work. The job took five weeks and was finally finished in January 1929. To get Perkins to Florida, Hemingway threatened to consider other publisher's offers. "If you don't come down and get it, you can't have it," Perkins quoted Hemingway as saying (Madison, 1966, Berg, 1978).

Perkins had to tell Scribner that there were three unprintable words in the manuscript.

> "What are they?" [Scribner] asked. Perkins, who never said more than "My God," found that he could not say them. "Write them, then," suggested Scribner. Perkins wrote out two of them on a sheet of paper. Scribner asked, "What's the third?" Perkins hesitated, and Scribner asked the question again, handing the pad back to him. After Perkins finally wrote it, Scribner looked at it and said, "Max, what would Hemingway think of you if he heard that you couldn't even write that word?" (Berg, 1978).

The more mythical variation has Perkins jotting the words down on his desk memo pad—supposedly "fuck," "shit" and "piss"—and being asked if it were necessary to include these under "Things to do today." This version is considered apocryphal, but good theater.

Hemingway rebelled against giving up "the full use of the language" in *Arms*. Perkins eventually swayed him with ego-soothing words: "If we can bring out this serial without arousing too serious objection, you will have enormously consolidated your position and will henceforth be further beyond objectionable criticism of a kind which is very bad because it prevents so many people from looking at the thing itself on its merits" (in Berg, 1978). The profanities were blanked out.

In addition to making Hemingway palpable to the public, Perkins was in charge of doing his tax return. He also set up a trust fund for Hemingway's family, and persuaded his company to increase the royalty on *Arms,* costing Scribner's several hundred dollars. His reasoning was that "We think the value of publishing for you is a great one in itself." He then suggested to Hemingway that he consider Scribner's suggestion of a minimum annual amount that he could absolutely count on. Hemingway went along with all of Perkins' generous offers except that one, because he knew that he could never work on salary (Berg, 1978).

In terms of morality, *Arms* did not fare much better than *Sun*. The second installment in *Scribner's* magazine was seized in Boston in July 1929. Hemingway wrote to Fitzgerald, worried that Scribner's would change their mind about publishing the book now, and Fitzgerald replied, "I wrote Max (not mentioning your letter) one of those don't-lose-your-head notes, though I, like you, never thot [sic] there was more than an outside chance of his being forced to let you down. I felt sure that if it came to a crisis he'd threaten to resign and force their hand" (in Bruccoli, 1978).

By 1930 Hemingway was without doubt Scribner's most successful author, obscenity notwithstanding. In the midst of the Depression, *Arms* was a number one best seller. Perkins wrote to Hemingway that the current economic conditions were "more likely to affect the general line of books—that it will surely affect—than so outstanding a book as *A Farewell*" (in Berg, 1978).

For Whom the Bell Tolls

When the Spanish Civil War broke out, Perkins knew that he could not keep Hemingway from throwing himself at danger once again. "If you had been there, and got out of it safely, what a story! But I wish you would not go to Spain...Anyhow, I hope you will let nothing prevent the publication of a novel in the spring" (Berg, 1978).

Beginning in March 1939, Hemingway worked steadily on *For Whom the Bell Tolls*, rewriting every day and doing final revisions on galley proofs. In first draft, he would not discuss his book with Perkins. He did tell him that he had turned down Hollywood offers and lecture tours, so he might need to draw on Scribner's financially. He offered collateral, although he assured Perkins that Scribner's would not need it (Baker, 1956; Berg, 1978).

As he wrote, he showed part of the novel to friends. His second wife, Pauline, now hated him so much that she would not look at it, which made Hemingway sad because he felt she had the best literary judgment of any of them (Baker, 1969).

Late in 1939 Perkins asked Hemingway to tell him "just a few of the elements in it to make a note from, and the title." In the beginning of the new year he received the first eight pages and 30 more from the middle. Perkins wired immediately:

MANAGER AS MUSE 137

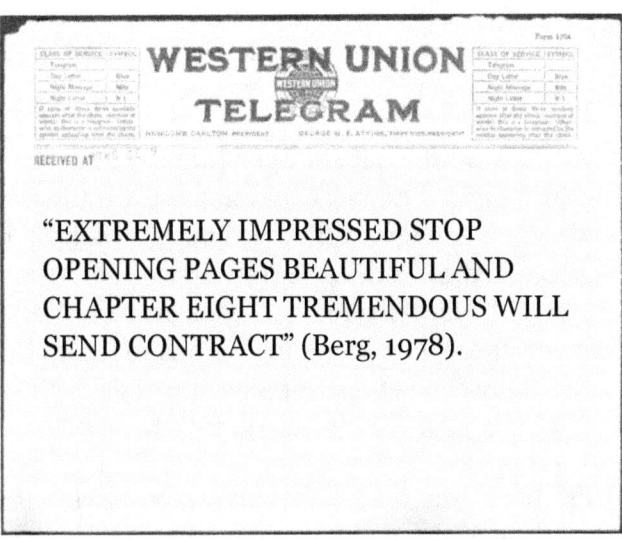

Perkins gave Hemingway an arbitrary deadline of April 1940, and Hemingway sent him the first 512 pages by then, with the title. Perkins wired,

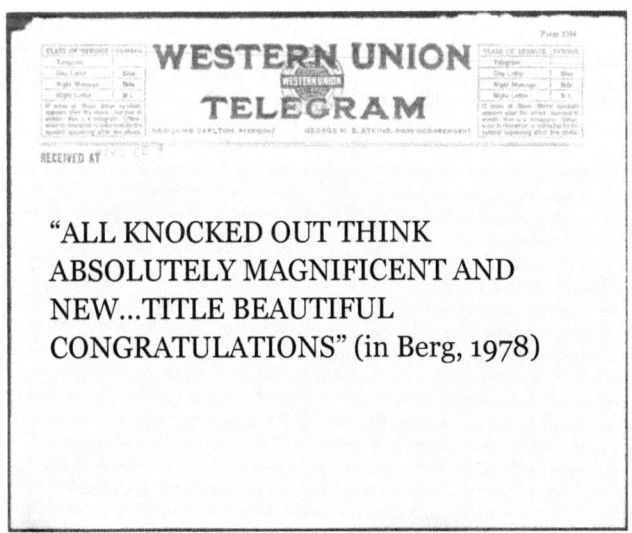

Perkins later remembered about the title choice, "Hemingway thought of a number of titles for his novel, but the first one he named to us was *For Whom the Bell Tolls,* and we immediately took it, thinking it could not be improved upon. It was his title

and it was right. This was true also of *A Farewell to Arms*. He had other titles, but there was no use even looking at them, for that one was so good" (Perkins, 1950).

But it was the ending that stumped him. Perkins felt Hemingway knew what it should be but could not get it into words (in Berg, 1978). When Hemingway finally figured out how to write the ending, he wired to Perkins on the first of July 1940, "BRIDGE ALL BLOWN." He delivered the book in New York adding the final touches there, handing it in sections to Perkins. Hemingway alternated between eavesdropping on Perkins' reading and "roistering" in a nearby hotel (Berg, 1978).

When the book was ready, Perkins wrote to Hemingway, "Now that everything is done that can be done and done magnificently on your part, I just want to say that I think that to have written this book in 15 months' time was miraculous. This hardly need be said, but you seemed to think that you had taken a very long time to do it" (Perkins, 1950).

In late August, Book of the Month chose *Bell* for its October selection, and offered to print 100,000. Scribner's matched that figure for the regular trade (Baker, 1969).

Thomas Wolfe

Writing to his mother from college, Wolfe said, "I am inevitable...I have genius" (Muller, 1947). From early in his career he felt he had talent, yet never quite learned what to do with it.

Thomas Wolfe was born in the mountains of Asheville, North Carolina, in 1900, a year that he felt was an omen for his inevitable fame. He was the last of seven children and was treated as his mother's favorite. He attended the University of North Carolina in accordance with his father's wishes, although he took an interest in playwriting instead of law. He went on to Harvard, with the help of an advance on his inheritance, to study playwriting with the famous George Baker's 47 Workshop, and stayed there for four years. After being graduated he took a teaching position at New York University where he taught on and off, interspersing trips to Europe when possible. On the way back from one of his European tours he met an older, married woman, Aline Bernstein, a well-known stage designer, who was to become one of the greatest influences on his life and work. Their stormy affair lasted for many years, and it was she who led him into the literary life in New York City and eventually to Maxwell Perkins.

If Perkins is known at all outside of the field of publishing it is for his work with Wolfe, especially their marathon editing of *Of Time and the River*, which Wolfe chronicled in a lecture, a series of articles, and eventual book, *The Story of a Novel*. For various reasons which have been disputed ever since, he left Perkins soon after this and signed with *Harper's*. After delivering his trunkful of manuscript to his new editor, Edward Aswell, Wolfe left on a trip to see the West. He contracted tubercular pneumonia and, after treatment in Seattle, was brought back to Johns Hopkins, where he died, aged 38. His work which was left behind was edited by his literary executor, Perkins, and Aswell, and published posthumously as *The Web and the Rock* and *You Can't Go Home Again*. The shortness of his life and the immensity of his work have made Wolfe a fertile subject for scholars. All aspects of his career, especially his relationships with his mentors—Baker, Bernstein, and Perkins—have been analyzed in detail (Berg, 1978; Holman, 1978; Nowell, 1960; Skipp, 1962).

One of Wolfe's outstanding characteristics was his size. He has best been described as being able to completely fill an average size doorway, standing six feet, seven inches, and gaining girth each year. Perkins and many others have pointed out how Wolfe never quite fit into life, and always felt as though he were a freak. Canby (1947) said, "An awkward man, shy, and always falling over furniture even when cold sober, he was a bull in anyone's china shop, yet clearly one of those vast personalities that emerge in dynamic times like the 1600s or the 1920s. What is reading time or conciseness to men like these?"

Wolfe's life can be seen as a journey from one mentor to another. Writing to his superintendent of schools in Asheville, about his first and favorite teacher, Margaret Roberts, he said, "I put the relationship of a fine teacher to a student just below the relation of a mother to her son and I don't think I could say more than this." While his unusual style invoked admiration and comment from all his teachers, the problems of his career as a professional writer were already evident when a Harvard professor wrote on his work: "The story sprawls a little—yet you can be terse and telling as you show again and again" (in Wolfe, 1946; Little, 1947).

At the same time Wolfe was writing to his mother regarding one of his early triumphs:

> Professor Baker read the prolog of my play...to the class a week ago. To my great joy he pronounced it the best prolog ever written here. The class, harshly critical as they usually are, were unanimous in praising it. This circumstance bewilders as well as pleases me. I am acutely no judge of my own work... The work over which I expend the most labor and care will fail to impress while other work, which I have written swiftly, almost without revision will score (Wolfe, 1943).

From the beginning Wolfe's reaction to even the slightest criticism was extreme. A fellow classmate describes the scene at a rehearsal of one of Wolfe's early Harvard plays:

> Baker stopped the rehearsal, turned to Tom and suggested that he would like to make such and such cuts ...Tom made a gesture of agreement, promptly followed by reasons why he felt the lines in question should be left in. Baker listened politely, then turned to the actors and read them the cuts. As he read, Tom, now sitting erect, began weaving back and forth in his chair like a polar bear suffering from the heat, and as Baker finished giving the cuts to the actors, Tom sprang to his feet with a tortured yell, and rushed out into the night...
>
> Ten or 15 minutes later, Tom walked in, quietly and casually, and took his seat...There was no further

reference to that cut, and no visible pain manifested by Tom when the scene [as cut] was played the next night. But this electrifying explosion, this leaping up, hands waving, with a bellow of distress, took place every time a cut was made for the first time. It began to be something we rather looked forward to (Barber, 1958).

It also was a scene repeated in various forms any time anyone tried to cut anything Wolfe wrote. The play in question, *Welcome to Our City,* was over four hours in length, in the cut version.

Wolfe's Major Works   **The books published by Wolfe include:**
Look Homeward, Angel (Scribner's, 1929)
Of Time and the River (Scribner's, 1935)
From Death to Morning (Scribner's, 1935), short stories
The Story of a Novel (Scribner's, 1936), non-fiction
The Web and the Rock (Harper & Brothers, 1939), posthumously, and
You Can't Go Home Again (Harper & Brothers 1940), posthumously.
Numerous stories and sections of his unpublished work were eventually brought out in magazines, journals, and other books.

There are many critics who argue that Wolfe was more a storyteller than a novelist and that his works are too autobiographical and full of rhetoric to be considered great. Many other Wolfe admirers, however, feel that Perkins ruined and restrained Wolfe's art. The controversy still rages among academics.

Work Habits

Wolfe's writing was emotional rather than intellectual. Probably no other American author drew so directly on his own experience and little else. His last editor, Aswell (1941), described the mental processes involved thus:

> Wolfe often said that he never learned anything except by experience, by trial and error...He had read many books and articles in which other writers told how they did it—and he found no help in them for himself...First and last his methods were his very own. He invented them—because he had to...He could not put anything...out of his consciousness until he had rehearsed it in memory a thousand times, going back over it again and again in every detail until he had got at the core of it and had extracted the last shred of meaning out of it on every level...His ingenious experiments with different ways of saying what he wanted to say, sometimes only worked out in his head, sometimes roughly sketched on paper... preceded the moment of spate writing and made it possible.

No two writers could be as different as Hemingway and Wolfe. Cunliffe (1964) points out, "The faults in Wolfe are those of Hemingway in reverse. Where Hemingway restricts his vocabulary to the point of penury, Wolfe errs towards prolixity; he succumbs to high-flown words like 'forever' and 'nevermore.' Where Hemingway suppressed emotion, Wolfe engulfs the reader in feeling."

The mechanics of the way Wolfe wrote changed slowly over his writing career. In his early New York days he used large bound ledgers, originally bought for him by Bernstein. He stood next to his icebox, just the right height for his gargantuan size. Later he would sit at a table and use ordinary sheets of manuscript paper, but a lot of them. Only about 90 of his handwritten words filled a sheet. As Cowley (1957) describes the scene,

> He wrote at top speed, never hesitating for a word, as though he were taking dictation. The moment a sheet was finished, he would push it aside without stopping to read it or even to number it. In the course of filling thousands of sheets with millions of words, he developed a wart on the middle finger of his right hand "almost as large and hard" he said in a letter, "but not as valuable, as a gambler's diamond."

Aswell (1941) describes Wolfe as writing as though he were "possessed."

> His first drafts were always done in longhand with a pencil, and when he had a secretary, as he did throughout his last year, one of her chores was to keep a dozen pencils sharpened and ready for his need. With amazing speed he would fill innumerable sheets of paper with his vigorous scrawl and toss them aside to fall on the floor for his secretary to pick up, put in order, and transcribe...The words came too fast for him, and in his effort to keep up with them he would often form only the first letter and last with a wriggle in between, so that only the initiated could decode his sentences.

Scholars have had trouble deciphering his notes, and Wolfe had trouble keeping secretaries.

Elizabeth Nowell (1960), his literary agent and biographer, who knew him from his early days at Scribner's, was of all people most privy to his private working habits during the successful years of his career. She completes the scene of a typical writing day:

> After perhaps an hour of striding up and down and talking to his secretary, he'd pull a chair up to his table,

roll up his sleeves, select a stub of pencil from the coffee can in which he kept them, light still another cigarette, and start to write, pursing his lips with concentration and occasionally running his fingers through his hair. From then on, almost without interruption, the sheets of yellow paper covered with his scrawl would fall like autumn leaves upon the floor, while his secretary scurried back and forth to pick them up and copy them.

Sometimes when he struck a difficult passage, he would seek out the seclusion of the bedroom, or of the kitchenette, where he would write quite comfortably standing up, with the top of the refrigerator for a table. Sometimes, especially in his later years, he would stride up and down, dictating directly to his secretary. He always wrote in iambic pentameter, and he would pace in time to his words, with one hand thrust, Napoleon-wise, between the buttons of his shirt to rub his chest, or with his hands hanging loosely at his sides while he clenched and unclenched his fingers with a sort of snapping noise.

But no matter where or how he wrote, the main thing was that he wrote—with no time out for lunch or rest or recreation from the middle of the morning till late afternoon when his exhausted secretary would finally insist on going home. Aswell says that in his later period Wolfe had gone in for much self-revision.

There would be at least two different versions of the same episode, sometimes four or five. When he was dissatisfied with a scene or character he would not...simply revise his draft and get it retyped: He would put it aside and rewrite it some different way from start to finish...small fragments became integral parts of larger fragments. Then they were salted away again to await the day when they would again be dug out and filled into still larger continuities (in Stevens, 1958).

Wolfe always referred to everything he wrote as "the book." "He did not know," reports Aswell (1941), "whether in the end it would make one book or a dozen, and he didn't much care. That seemed to him the publisher's problem, and he was right about it." This has led some critics to discount Wolfe as a novelist. They consider his work to be "merely selections by his editors from his journals and his autobiographical outpourings," as Skipp (1962) said. One described his books not as individual works but as parts of one big autobiography.

As described by the *New York Times*, "Wolfe poured out his words by the million and let the best words win." One of his fellow faculty members at NYU said that he could "no more use a blue pencil on his writings than a father could sacrifice his first born" (Skipp, 1962; Middlebrook, 1947). In other words, Wolfe lacked a crucial writer's characteristic—the inner critic.

When visiting the National Gallery about 1935 when his career was at its peak, Wolfe noted in his personal notebook:

> It is a curious thing how people...are instantly convinced that the proper thing to do with any piece of writing is to "cut"—"cut ruthlessly"—"be relentless"—"don't spare yourself" etc. It seems to be taken as a fundamental axiom of artistic truth that any book that exceeds 300 pages should be "cut to the bone" and the result will eventually be a marked improvement. Why is this?... This conviction applies only to the art of writing. A man who waded into the paintings of Turner, or... Rubens...with a blue pencil and a pair of shears, saying "You don't need this, old boy—much too much of that—slash!—the end," etc.—... would be regarded as a maniac and a dangerous criminal, but when the same thing is done to a man's book... the act is represented as one of noble virtue—and the only pity is he didn't do more of it, etc. (in Skipp, 1962).

Today, he would be a prolific blogger.

In one of his letters to a writing friend, Wolfe describes a scene where his agents were at his house "ransacking manuscripts in search of new material. Most of it was dismissed with polite regrets as 'not a story, whatever that means—I've never been able to find out myself'" (in Skipp, 1962).

Indeed the only way his work was ever published as stories was through the efforts of Perkins, his agent and others to lift certain self-contained sequences from "the book" and offer them to periodicals for publication.

Relationship with Perkins

After Wolfe's death, a torn fragment among his unsent papers included this note to Perkins: "In all my life, until I met you, I never had a friend" (in Berg, 1978).

From the moment they met, the Perkins-Wolfe relationship became publishing myth. Stories reported that his first manuscript was brought to Scribner's in a trunk and was returned, after being edited, in a taxi. The legend appeared in print when *Of Time and the River* was published, although it had been circulating since the publication of *Look Homeward, Angel*. About the time of *River*, *Publisher's Weekly*, the primary trade journal, reported in an article on Perkins entitled, "Laurels to an Editor":

> It is a tribute to his publisher that Mr. Wolfe should make the Scribner office his second home and it is a tribute to both author and publisher that the relations should be so friendly after the desperate struggle to reduce both *Look Homeward, Angel* and *Of Time and the River* to a bulk sufficiently small to allow them to be put between covers (in Skipp, 1962).

Many of the legends have some fact in them, but most exaggerate—a bit—Wolfe's output and make his editors more heroic than they were. As Skipp (1962) says, "Neither the rate and amount of Wolfe's production, nor the role his editors played need to be exaggerated to meet standards for heroism."

Ten years after the author's death, the *Saturday Review* ran an article about Wolfe, including a facsimile of a manuscript page with penciled revisions on it. The caption read, "For a sample of Mr. Perkins' editing, the reader is referred to the illustration on the opposite page." However, the revisions were in Wolfe's handwriting, which was not pointed out until nine months later when one of Wolfe's biographers and friends wrote to the magazine. The impression, however, was already made that Perkins had directly corrected and changed Wolfe's text, which is not true (Skipp, 1962).

Perkins did spend an enormous amount of time with Wolfe and both cared for each other deeply. Wolfe eventually left Scribner's for many reasons, some unexplained, which will be discussed later. When a book as large and as important as *River* was in Scribner's, an enormous amount of resources were directed toward its publication. Wheelock, in fact, was in charge of all the final copyediting and proofs of Wolfe's books (Nowell, 1960).

In 1928 Wolfe was in Europe, already sure that he was a failure as a playwright and convinced he would be a failure as a novelist as well. His agent, Madeline Boyd, sent the manuscript of *Angel* to Perkins, who wrote later, "The first time I heard of Thomas Wolfe I had a sense of foreboding. I who loved the man say this. Every good thing that comes is accompanied by trouble" (in Madison, 1966; Berg, 1978).

But as they worked through *Angel*, it became apparent to many of those observing the relationship that this was an editorial marriage made in heaven. As their friendship deepened, they would take long walks through New York City together, Wolfe talking about future projects. When he would stop talking, Perkins would make up ideas for books, just meandering until something would catch Wolfe's attention (Berg, 1978).

During the year of publication of his first novel, Wolfe wrote to his agent about his new editor: "I have the greatest respect and liking for him. My faith is too simple but I believe he can do almost everything to make a book go." Perkins began to feel uncomfortable about this adulation, but he understood Wolfe enough to know that he felt as though he were a freak. Not just physically to the world, but also to his family because he was writer (Berg, 1978).

As Berg (1978) says,

> He still seemed to his family to be doing something queer—something that really wasn't work in their opinion. As an artist, Wolfe was made to feel like a one-eyed monster. That someone should have befriended him made him excessive in his gratitude and devotion to his protector, but blind to any dangers in their working together.

Wolfe wrote to Perkins at this time, "The name 'Scribner's' naturally makes a warm glow in my heart, but you are chiefly 'Scribner's' to me: You have done what I had ceased to believe one person could do for another—you have created liberty and hope for me...You are one of the rocks to which my life is anchored (in Berg, 1978).

After *Angel* was published, Wolfe went off to Switzerland to work on his next book, sending "scribblings," in Berg's word, to his editor,

> constantly asking for comments and approval. His notes added up to almost book length themselves, and they mostly dealt with the tone, attitude, structure and character of his planned work... [At his second book's

core] much like a kernel from the beginning, but unrevealed until much later, would be the idea of man's quest for his father [an idea Perkins had casually suggested on one of their walks] (in Berg, 1978).

Perkins kept up his usual stream of encouraging letters: "When you get down to work, just do the work the best you can. Don't ever think about the public, or the critics, or any of those things. You are a born writer if there ever was one and have no need to worry about whether this new book will be as good as the *Angel*" (Perkins, 1950).

Perkins was less successful in his attempt to get two of his favorite writers to like each other. He had Wolfe meet Fitzgerald in Paris the summer after *Angel,* and Wolfe, the poor country boy, did not care for the rich city kid who threw money around (Berg, 1978).

Upset by some minor negative reviews, feeling hounded by Bernstein and other literati, Wolfe decided in Europe to give up writing altogether. He wrote from Geneva, "I shall not write any more books and since I must begin to make other plans for the future, I should like to know how much money I will have. I want to thank you and Scribner's for your kindness to me, and I shall hope someday to resume and continue a friendship which has meant a great deal to me" (in Berg, 1978).

Perkins tried not to believe that this would really be true, and wrote back, "If I really believed you would be able to stand by your decision, your letter would be a great blow to me...If anyone were ever destined to write, that one is you...The reviews—and I must have seen all the really important ones—were very fine" (Perkins, 1950).

In return he received silence, so the editor wrote again. "If you do not write me some good news soon, I shall have to start out on a spying expedition myself," and "For heaven's sake, send us some word." Eventually Perkins received a radiogram from Germany:

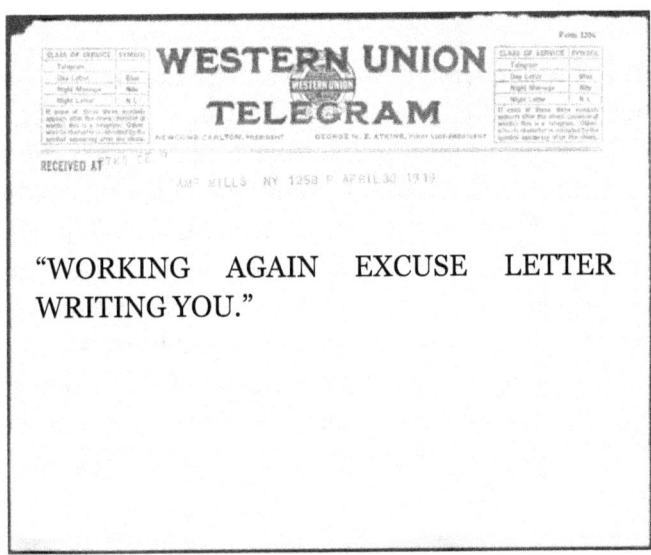

"WORKING AGAIN EXCUSE LETTER WRITING YOU."

This was followed by a wire in October, two months after he had chucked the profession:

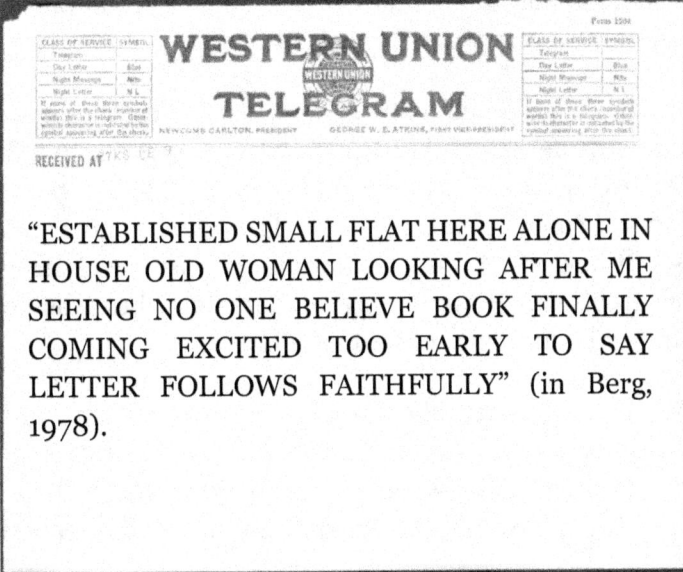

"ESTABLISHED SMALL FLAT HERE ALONE IN HOUSE OLD WOMAN LOOKING AFTER ME SEEING NO ONE BELIEVE BOOK FINALLY COMING EXCITED TOO EARLY TO SAY LETTER FOLLOWS FAITHFULLY" (in Berg, 1978).

"God knows what I would do without [Max]," Wolfe wrote in 1934. But he had also begun to take up Marxism and become more socially conscious. He was later to use the political differences between the two as justification for the final break up (Reeves, 1958).

On returning to the United States, Wolfe found that he could not work and was on the verge of physical and mental illness. He asked Perkins to find him a quiet place to live near Manhattan where he could work in almost complete isolation for the next three months. He also asked for more emotional help: "I am not asking you to cure me of my sickness, because you can't do that. I must do it myself, but I am very earnestly asking you to help me to do certain things that will make my cure easier and less painful." He then described his problems with Bernstein in painful detail. He explained that his love problems were the reason that his letters from Europe had all sounded "unhappy" (Berg, 1978).

Perkins replied as a true friend. "I'll do anything you ask of me and any reluctance will come only from lack of confidence to do good...I'm generally horribly lonely [in the summer]. There are people enough, but none I really care to see. I'll count on some of your company, anyway" (in Berg, 1978).

Perkins tried to help him with his book, but he knew he could not help him with Bernstein. "I can't seem to," he wrote to a friend, "perhaps because I never had trouble comparable to what he has had. And so I can't feel what he does. Then too he and I are really friends, but he doesn't think I know much." Wolfe was struggling to break free from the influence of Bernstein, but was coming more under the influence of Perkins (Berg, 1978).

Since Wolfe's best mode of expression was the written word, and he stammered when excited, he wrote Perkins long, rhetorical letters, detailing exactly what he was thinking and feeling more intimately than he would have revealed to anyone in person. He told Perkins that he thought of him as "a high class gentleman," the phrase he used as a child for those he looked up to (Berg, 1978).

Throughout the next year or so the relationship tilted—the father confessor helping the struggling young artist get through that bane of all successful novelists, the second book. By the end of 1932, Wolfe wrote Perkins making it clear that he had left town without telling anyone, including Perkins, where he had gone. Perkins wrote back, hoping his letter would find him, passing on the enthusiasm of his other author, Hemingway: "He is simply wild about your writing, and he wants to see you...He says the only thing he is afraid of is that you will quarrel with him" (in Skipp, 1962; Berg, 1978).

Perkins wrote to Fitzgerald that, "Even if one had an utterly free hand, instead of being subject to constant abuse (with [accusations of] God damned Harvard English, groveling at the feet of Henry James, etc.), it would be a matter of editing inside sentences even, and that would be a dangerous business." He felt Wolfe's writing would mature on its own. "It's not that he thinks he's better than anyone else. He just does not think about the other people at all. When he reads them he is quite keen about them for a while, but they do not seem important to him because what he is doing seems to him momentous" (in Berg, 1978).

Perkins also arranged for Wolfe and Hemingway to meet, thinking Wolfe would benefit. "I brought it about," he told Wolfe's biographer, John Skally Terry, "because I hoped Hemingway would be able to influence Tom to overcome his faults in writing...such as his tendency to repetitions and excessive expressions." Hemingway passed on his dictum to "break off when you are going good—Then you can rest easily and on the next day easily resume." Perkins told Terry that Hemingway "can be blunt, but he can also be more gentle in speech than anyone I know. He wanted to help Tom, and everything went well, except I think Tom was not in the least affected." For his part Hemingway felt Wolfe had "magnificent talent and a delicate spirit," in Berg's (1978) words, but he knew Perkins was doing a lot of Wolfe's thinking. "He cautioned Perkins not to lose Tom's confidence, for the author's sake" (in Berg, 1978).

Perkins knew how difficult it is for a writer to write that second book, and he was worried that his most promising young author was exhausted. "Max was also worried that, if Wolfe continued writing," Skipp (1962) said, "his book could never be contained within two covers. It was already four times as long as the uncut manuscript of *Look Homeward, Angel,* over ten times the length of most novels. And Wolfe was adding 50,000 words a month."

He sent along to Wolfe an invitation to be visiting novelist at the Colorado Writers' Conference in July of that year. It paid $250 for ten days, and Perkins felt that this would bring him home to finish the collection of short stories they were working on. Wolfe wired, "ACCEPT COLORADO OFFER RETURN EARLY JUNE NO TITLE STORIES YET...WAIT FOR ME" (in Berg, 1978).

Perkins allowed for a period of adjustment after Wolfe returned to the States, not wishing to rush him into work on the proofs of the collection. But he was also worried that Wolfe would stretch out his travels and postpone publication of the stories. This made him continue to urge Wolfe to get to work on the stories before he left for the West (Berg, 1978).

Perkins' fears were realized. He received postcards and letters detailing Wolfe's journeys, meetings with Edna Ferber, Dorothy Parker, and Hollywood agents. Perkins responded with reminders about the proofs, and Wolfe responded with more postcards and anecdotes. From the West he wrote,

> You must not put the manuscript...in final form until after my return to New York. If that means the book...will have to be deferred until next spring, then it will have to be deferred, but I will not consent this time to allow the

book to be taken away from me and printed and published until I myself have had time to look at the proofs, and at any rate to talk to you about certain revisions, changes, excisions, or additions that ought to be made. I really mean this, Max. I have money enough to live on for a while now (in Skipp, 1962).

In August Perkins wrote to him, "I have been through the stories and I think they are very fine stories. They show how objective you can be, and how varied you can be, and I was looking at the book from that point of view considerably. It would be an answer to what you have had in adverse criticism. It is a fine book. But I'll wait and argue with you when you come back, over a glass of Coca-Cola" (Perkins, 1950).

Wolfe replied from Hollywood that Perkins should think about the sequence of the stories, so that their unity would be enhanced and the title, *From Death to Morning,* justified. He concluded with, "Yes, I know I've stayed too long, but Max, Max, you must wait on me—I've got to see San Francisco...Don't take the book away before I get back" (Perkins, 1950).

It is obvious from his letters that Wolfe was still very distressed that Perkins had "taken" *Of Time and the River* away from him. He was not going to let it happen again. This contributed to the growing rift between them. The fact that Perkins was contemplating doing this a second time indicates that his opinion of Wolfe's professionalism had declined also. To Perkins' amazement, when Wolfe returned later that month, he corrected the proofs quickly and with no fuss. Within one month the book of stories was published. This was to be the last work Wolfe would ever do with Scribner's (Skipp, 1962; Berg, 1978).

After the short story collection was published, Wolfe did not know what to work on. He met with Perkins and his wife one night in November for one drink, but Wolfe never had only one drink. He became his usual abusive drunken self and showed up at Perkins' office the next afternoon apologizing. He said he must start working again and Perkins must help him decide what to work on. Perkins agreed to meet him in the middle of an East River bridge where there would be no alcohol to mar their conversation. Perkins remembered later, "Tom had a strange distrust of himself which made him apparently actually believe that no other publisher would take him, and he often intimated that he would leave us, but I think merely to observe my reaction" (in Berg, 1978).

During the stormier years of their relationship, however, even when Wolfe was vacillating on his decision to leave Scribner's, Perkins remained his loyal friend and supporter. In the summer of 1937, when Wolfe was on a sudden and extended trip home to North Carolina, Perkins wrote to an author-friend,

> I took the risk of paying a month's rent on [an] apartment because the agent has been threatening to dispossess him at any moment, for the last week, and I did not know what in the world would happen if all his manuscripts were thrown out on the sidewalk, or even put up for auction—which I believe the landlord is entitled to do, to the extent of the debt. Miss Nowell has been telegraphing and writing Tom, but has got no answer...I thought it would do Tom lots of good to get back into the mountains, but perhaps the great fame that he enjoys there, and the happiness of being among his own people, has not enabled him to work properly. It must have done him good in resting him, and I suppose John Barleycorn is not so ubiquitous in that region as this (Perkins, 1950).

In Wolfe's last illness, Perkins wrote his softly encouraging letters that required no answers:

> Don't get impatient about loss of time. You don't really lose time, in the ordinary sense. Even six months would

not be important. Even if you were really relaxing, as they call it, all that time, you would be getting good from it, even as a writer. I hope you will manage to do it, too. I could send you some good books to read, but I don't think you will want to do any reading yet for a while. What you ought to do is to realize that by really resting now, you are in fact actually gaining time, not losing it (Perkins, 1950).

After Wolfe's death, Perkins kept hearing a line from Lear, "He hates him that would upon the rack of this tough world stretch him out longer" (Berg, 1978). He wrote later in *Carolina* magazine:

[Tom] was wrestling as no artist in Europe would have to do with the material of literature—a great country not yet revealed to its own people. It was not as with English artists who revealed England to Englishman through generations, each one accepting what was true from his predecessors, in a gradual accretion, through centuries. Tom...knew that the light and color of America were different; that the smells and sounds, its people, and all the structure and dimensions of our continent were unlike anything before. It was with this that he was struggling, and it was that struggle alone that, in a large sense, governed all he did...He had to fit his body to the doorways, vehicles, and furnishings of smaller men, so he had to fit his expression to the conventional requirements of a space and time that were as surely too small for his nature as they were for his subject (in Berg, 1978).

As Wolfe's literary executor, Perkins agreed to the sale of Wolfe's letters for publication, not for the money but to make the materials available to writers and scholars. He felt this was important for his stature as a writer, but of his popularity he had no doubt. He told Bernstein that Wolfe would always be read because "there will always be a generation of sophomores to discover and delight in him" (in Berg, 1978).

Wolfe's own account of his experience in writing his second book, recounted in *The Story of a Novel,* evoked much reaction from critics. One of the most severe and least distinguished was a virtually unknown writer, Jack Woodford, who wrote a book for writers called *Why Write a Novel.* In it he included this description:

> You will never believe me when I tell you this, but I can prove it. One American editor's pride and joy today is that he threw a lot of the Immortal work of Tom Wolfe into the wastebasket. What a distinction for him to go down the ages upon: "Who am I? Why, fellows, I am the guy who took from the world a hell of a lot of what Tom Wolfe wrote because I didn't like it." The same thing would have happened to Tom Wolfe in any publishing house, and at the hands of any editor; BUT EACH EDITOR WOULD HAVE TAKEN AWAY A <u>DIFFERENT PART</u> OF TOM WOLFE...Because Tom Wolfe at the time was helpless to prevent this sabotage upon his work. He was too young a writer...Tom Wolfe is dead now. Everyone concedes that he was a great genius. Before he died it was a standing joke in New York editorial offices that he drove up to his publisher's office in a truck and unloaded his novels by the pound. Editors derided him and smeared him because he made his novels longer than it was thought they ought to be; whereupon the overplus was thrown into the wastebasket...Ask yourself what these same editors' with their blue pencils would have done to Shakespeare; to Shelly (in Skipp, 1962).

This disgruntled author's critique is of interest primarily because of Perkins' response, one of the few times he ever responded directly to this sort of criticism. He was more upset about the view it gave of editors than that it would harm his reputation:

I got a copy of your [book] because I heard it contained a furious attack upon me. It does, and one that is plainly libelous, as Tom Wolfe's own letters alone will show. But I found the book such good reading upon the whole that I suppose I now shall read it through. And I'll enjoy it, for the most part. But I am the slowest reader in the world, and so hardly ever get to read anything but what we are publishing. Which is a very bad thing in an editor...

As for the greater part of Tom Wolfe's manuscripts being torn out and thrown into the waste basket, it is not true. Not a page was thrown into the wastebasket...Almost nothing of what Tom wrote failed to appear in print except much that was so unfinished, as he himself thought that it could not be published. But that too would have been revised by Tom and would have appeared, if Tom had lived.

As for Tom not being in a position to resist sabotage, why not? He had a contract. We were bound to publish everything he wrote except what was libelous and obscene...The truth is that nothing was ever taken from Tom's writings without his full consent...Tom <u>demanded</u> help. He had to have it...

Then you speak of fun being poked at Tom because of the hugeness of his manuscripts—because he delivered a packing case from a truck. In fact, it was a taxicab. You say he was ridiculed. To my knowledge, he was not. He was admired...Anyhow, from what I have read of the rest of your book...you have said many right and true things that have not been said before. Editors aren't much, and can't be. They can only help a writer realize himself, and they can ruin him if he's pliable, as Tom was not. That is why the editors I know shrink from tampering with a manuscript and do it only when it is required of them by the author, as it was by Tom. When an editor gets to think differently from that, to think he knows more about a writer's book than the writer —and some do—he is dead, done for, and dangerous (Perkins, 1950).

A Perkins' critic, however, Lynn (1978), in an article entitled, "The Strange Unhappy Life of Maxwell Perkins," faults both editor and author:

> The incredible editorial effort that Perkins brought to bear upon the chaos of Wolfe's manuscripts and his unending willingness to put up with Wolfe's egomania, foul temper, and treachery had nothing to do with the publishing business, in the final analysis. Perkins did not merely collaborate with the author,...he adopted him...As Wolfe's literary agent Elizabeth Nowell, recalled "He all but lived at Perkins' house as a member of the family—or as Perkins' son which to all intents and purposes he was. Perkins never seemed to see enough of him."

Those who felt that Perkins acted appropriately for an editor often came back to a point made by Thomas Lyle Collins in *Sewanee Review* in 1942: "If the novel had not been there in the first place, no editor's pencil could have brought it to light."

On the other extreme from the Perkins critics are the Perkins idolizers, mostly his writers. Chief among these was Struthers Burt, who claimed boldly in the *Saturday Review* in 1951 that Perkins "was a greater genius than the author." He went on to make a statement which caused even more controversy:

> Now I will say something that has never before been said publicly. But it is time it was said in the interest of truth and literary history and in order to set the record straight. There is not the slightest question in the minds of the few who knew Max Perkins intimately that the Tom Wolfe episode killed him. Exactly from the date of Tom's betrayal he began to die (Burt, 1951).

The fact that Perkins did not die until nine years later was pointed out by many of his friends who wrote to the *Saturday Review*, but Burt stood by his claim in rebutting them.

Perkins himself had defended his work with his author in an article, unfinished at his death, published in the *Harvard Library Bulletin*. "There never was any cutting that Tom did not agree to. He knew that cutting was necessary. His whole impulse was to utter what he felt and he had no time to revise and compress" (Perkins, 1947).

Look Homeward, Angel

In the early twenties, Wolfe wrote to a friend, "I have finished a very full and complete outline of my book—the outline itself the length almost of a novel—and at present I am writing about 3,000 words a day, which I hope to increase to 4,000. The novel will be Dickensian or Meredithian in length, but the work of cutting—which means, of course, adding an additional 50,000 words—must come later" (Skipp, 1962).

Bernstein was the first to help Wolfe get his manuscript published. She took *O Lost!*, as it was then called, to Boni and Liveright, but after considering it for five weeks, they declined. "It is so long—so terribly long—that it is most difficult for a reader to sustain an interest to the end. One cannot deny that much of it has quality, if not originality—on the whole it is a pattern—the autobiography of a young man—and so much of it has been done, and so often, that we hesitate to take another chance." This brought on one of the famous Wolfe depressions (Reeves, 1965).

Sloane (1938) goes on to detail how Wolfe's agent, Madeleine Boyd, got the manuscript to Perkins in a roundabout way. When she would come to call on him on other business she would talk about the book and its author. Finally Perkins asked why she would not let him see it. "Editors, she felt, were impatient, and you couldn't be impatient with a genius like Wolfe. She admitted, also, that the first 100,000 words were not up to the rest of the book. So," as Sloane describes it, "if Mr. Perkins wanted to see the script he would have to promise to read every word. He did—perhaps without fully realizing just how many words there were—and when the manuscript arrived he stuck by his promise."

Perkins, however, did not find himself so enthralled that he read it straight through at one sitting. He found the beginning intriguing, but then Wolfe characteristically veered off into autobiographical material and Perkins lost interest. He gave the manuscript to another Scribner's editor, thinking, in Berg's words, "Here is another promising novel that probably will come to nothing." More than a week later the other editor came in and showed Perkins another exceptional scene, and that brought the editor back to the book and his promise (Berg, 1978).

He recognized the talent and the potential, but he was leery of the obstacles to publication. It was "very strong meat." There would also be a lot of reorganization and cutting. Perkins thought he should find out about the author first hand before beginning another fight with Scribner's to publish it (Berg, 1978), so he wrote to Wolfe in Vienna:

> Mrs. Ernest Boyd left with us, some weeks ago, the manuscript of your novel, *O Lost*. I do not know whether it would be possible to work out a plan by which it might be worked into a form publishable by us, but I do know that, setting the practical aspects of the matter aside, it is a very remarkable thing, and that no editor could read it without being excited by it and filled with admiration by many passages in it and sections of it (Perkins, 1950).

As Berg (1978) says, even then, "Max worried about the two 'Moby Dicks' he would have to restrain—the man even more than the book." After Wolfe described their first meeting in a "breathless" letter to his first mentor, Roberts:

I was taken to [Perkins'] office where I found Mr. Charles Scribner (simply there, I think, to take a look at me, for he withdrew immediately saying he would leave us alone). Mr. Perkins is not at all "Perkinsy"—name sounds Mid-western but he is Harvard man, probably New England family, early forties, but looks younger, very elegant and gentle in dress and manner. He saw I was nervous and excited, spoke to me quietly, told me to take off coat and sit down...

He mentioned a certain short scene in the book, and in my eagerness and excitement I burst out, "I know you can't print that! I'll take it out at once, Mr. Perkins." "Take it out?" he said. "It's one of the greatest short stories I have ever read." He said he had been reading it to Hemingway the week before...

I saw now that Perkins had a great batch of notes in his hand and that on the desk was a great stack of handwritten paper—a complete summary of my whole enormous book. I was so moved and touched to think that someone at length had thought enough of my work to sweat over it in this way that I almost wept...Said finally if I was hard up he thought Scribner's would advance money...A few days later the second meeting—I brought notes along as to how I proposed to set to work...When I asked him if I could say something definite to a dear friend [Bernstein], he smiled and said he thought so; that their minds were practically made up; that I should get to work immediately and that I should have a letter from him in a few days. As I went prancing out I met Mr. Wheelock who took me by the hand and said, "I hope you have a good place to work in—you have a big job ahead."

...For the first time in my life I was getting criticism I could really use—the scenes he wanted cut or changed were invariably the least essential and the least interesting—all the scenes that I had thought too coarse, vulgar, profane or obscene for publication he forbade me to touch save for a word or two—there was one as rough as anything in Elizabethan drama—when I spoke of this he said it was a masterpiece, and that he had been reading it to Hemingway (in Burlingame, 1946).

"It was the first time, so far as I can remember," he said later, "that anyone had concretely suggested to me that anything I had written was worth as much as 15 cents." The contract gave Wolfe 10% of the first 2,000 copies and 15% after that, with an advance of $500 (Berg, 1978, Madison, 1966). In another letter to Roberts, he confessed

> Mr. Perkins and Wheelock warned me not to go too much with "that Algonquin crowd"—the Hotel Algonquin is where most of the celebrities waste their time and admire one another's cleverness. This also makes me laugh. I am several million miles away from these mighty people, and at the present time want to get no closer (Wolfe, 1946)

From January to August of 1929, Wolfe did get closer, by working hard on revising and whittling *O Lost* into *Look Homeward, Angel*.

Perkins was thrilled with Wolfe's writing, but not with the result of his cutting. Although Wolfe made many of the suggested deletions, the new transitions lengthened it so much that the net effect was a loss of only eight pages (Berg, 1978, Skipp, 1962).

Legend notwithstanding, the actual size of *O Lost!* was 1,114 pages, 2¼ reams high, about five inches, 330,000 words long. Skipp's (1962) analysis of the typescript shows that 147 cuts were made which took out 7,900 lines or 95,000 words. 16 passages, equaling 5,000 words were added. Only one important transposition of material from one part to another was made.

As he tried to cut, it became clear that Wolfe was unable to "distinguish between the superfluous and the essential" (Skipp, 1962). He wrote to his sister,

> We are cutting out big chunks...and my heart bleeds to see it go, but it's die dog or eat the hatchet...We will have a shorter book and one easier to read when we finish...This man Perkins is a fine fellow and perhaps the best publisher's editor in America. I have great confidence in him and I usually yield to his judgment (in Berg, 1978).

Although the editors suggested the cuts, Wolfe wrote the transitions, working with his editors until the page proof stage. The deadline was comfortably met—a first and last for Wolfe. No part was taken out without mutual consent; no pages went "into the wastebasket." Wolfe saved every piece and Perkins suggested he would be able to use all of it again (Skipp, 1962; Berg, 1978).

Skipp's (1962) analysis of the cuts shows that most were made "as much from considerations of literary merit as for publishing expediency." His analysis clearly shows that Perkins' motive in cutting, at least the first Wolfe book, was in improving the novel as a unified work of art (Berg, 1978).

Years later Perkins wrote to one of his writers, "I remember the horror with which I realized when working with Tom Wolfe on his manuscript of *The Angel,* that all these people were almost completely real, that the book was literally autobiographical...He said, 'But you don't understand. I think they are great people'" (Perkins, 1950).

As they moved closer to publication, Perkins confessed that he did not like the title, *O Lost!* Wolfe submitted a list, from which Perkins and Wheelock chose their favorite, which turned out to be Wolfe's also, a phrase from Milton's *Lycidas, Look Homeward, Angel* (Berg, 1978).

After publication, in October 1929, Wolfe's agent, Boyd, explained to Perkins that he had really wanted to dedicate the book to his editor. "But his friend Aline Bernstein who sent him to us, has first claims. So I told him I was sure you would not mind waiting for another one. I only wanted you to know...how grateful he is, and how he understands what he owes to your kindness, patience and understanding" (Berg, 1978).

Two months after publication, when the book had found its way, Wolfe wrote to his new friend as well as editor:

> One year ago I had little hope for my work, and I did not know you. What has happened since may seem to be only a modest success to many people; but to me it is touched with strangeness and wonder. It is a miracle...I can no longer think of the time I wrote [Angel], but rather of the time when you first talked to me about it, and when you worked upon it (in Berg, 1978).

Fitzgerald read the book in 20 consecutive hours, much impressed by it and the author, whom he had just met. He wired Wolfe that he was "enormously moved and grateful" and wrote to their mutual editor, "You have a great find in him—what he'll do is incalculable" (in Berg, 1978).

Wolfe took off for Europe in 1930 and began receiving glowing reviews upon the British publication of the novel. Unfortunately the British publisher, Frere-Reeves, made the mistake of sending him some not-so-good ones as well. Wolfe called them "dirty, distorted, and full of mockery" (Berg, 1978).

Berg (1978) points out the book's significance in Perkins' career as well:

> By the time Angel was published, Max Perkins had redrawn the artistic boundaries of his profession. Before Perkins, editors had almost nothing to do with writers until they submitted their final manuscripts. Max, however, understood that writers often need help before

a book was all on paper rather than after. He had an uncanny sixth sense of just when an author was lagging and just how to prod him along. Inevitably, he became enmeshed in his writer's personal lives.

Of Time and the River

"I am aching with a new book," Wolfe wrote to an NYU colleague. "I loathe the idea of not writing it, and I loathe the idea of writing it—I am lazy, and doing a book is agony—60 cigarettes a day, 20 cups of coffee, miles of walking and flying about, nightmares, nerves, madness—there are better ways, but this, God help me, is mine" (Volkening, 1939).

After the publication of *Angel,* Wolfe was faced with the same problem that plagues all first novelists—the second novel. For years afterwards he piled up thousands of words, with no plan, that only a publisher and editor like Scribner's and Perkins could turn into a book (Skipp, 1962).

He eventually abandoned the procedure he had used on *Angel* of writing chapter by chapter chronologically. His method now became the one he would use for the rest of his life, as Skipp (1962) describes the process:

> He began on any day simply to write that episode in his past that flooded in upon him most strongly and irresistibly. He might then proceed to the end of the episode, or he might...set that episode until a later time. The only relation that the episodes he developed in this way bore to one another was the inescapable one that they all fitted somewhere into the mosaic of his life.

Perkins and Wolfe at this time took walks, with the editor dropping casual hints and suggestions for a novel. One stuck, as Perkins described to a Wolfe admirer;

> I said to Tom that I had always thought a grand story could be written about a boy who had never seen his

father, his father having left when he was a baby, or even before that, as a soldier of fortune say,—and of how this boy set out to find his father and went through a series of adventures...and finally did find him in some odd situation. I just said this idly for of course such a story I was thinking of could not be written by one of those fairy tale writers that we all publish (Berg, 1978).

"I think I could use that, Max," Wolfe had said. Perkins was a little worried that Wolfe would even consider such a trite story until he realized that Wolfe was "taking the search for a father in a profound sense, and that is what he was bound to write." For the next four years, that is what he tried to write (Berg, 1978).

Perkins suggested that Wolfe apply for a grant from the Guggenheim Foundation so he could quit teaching at NYU and have the security to work abroad for a year. Bernstein was upset and felt that Perkins did this to get Wolfe away from her, which was the eventual consequence. With the help of Perkins' recommendation, Wolfe received the fellowship and Perkins arranged a $4,500 advance from Scribner's to be paid in monthly installments. Combined with the royalties from *Angel,* Wolfe had $10,000 and no longer had to rely on Bernstein for financial support (Berg, 1978).

From Switzerland that year, 1930, Wolfe wrote: "Now, the general movement of the book is from the universal to the individual" (in Skipp, 1962). Another letter he wrote to Perkins was never mailed:

> You're the only person I've got left to look to...but I am a complete exile and solitary on the face of the earth: It is the simple God's truth. I want to write you about the book—I think that it's all bound together now, and an idea hovers over the whole thing that thrills me. You gave me the idea once and I've never forgotten it (in Skipp, 1962).

The letter he mailed to Perkins said:

> I want to tell you finally that I am not in <u>despair</u> over the book. I have worked on—I am in <u>doubt</u> about it—and I am not sure about anything: I think I will finish it, I think it may be valuable and fine—or it may be worthless (in Skipp, 1962).

Wolfe was reading the Old Testament as an example of great literature, including Perkins' own favorite part, Ecclesiastes. He told his editor that it belonged "to the mightiest poetry that was ever written—and the narrative passages in the Old Testament...make the narrative style of any modern novelist look puny." He chose one phrase for a legend on the title page of one section of his book: "One generation passeth away, and another cometh: But the earth abideth forever." Hemingway had earlier used this and the next few lines for the epitaph of *The Sun Also Rises* (Berg, 1978).

Perkins was encouraging but worried that at even this early date the book was getting away from its author, writing, "It sounds like a very Leviathan of a book as you describe it, now lying in the depths of your consciousness...and I believe you are the man who can draw out such a Leviathan" (in Berg, 1978).

Finally Perkins' suggestions began to take hold in his creative mind: "I had this vast amount of material, and what you said began to give shape to it." He also gave a new title to his work in progress: "The October Fair or Time and the River: A Vision" (in Berg, 1978).

Perkins replied right away, "Every time you write about the book I get as excited as I did when I began *The Angel*. I wish to thunder you would come back with the manuscript." At the same time, Wolfe was noting in his personal ledger: "Mr. Perkins, I suppose you think I have been plainspoken enough...—but I have not begun yet. On the contrary, I have always had a partial reserve in speaking to you, I have hinted at things, and got at them indirectly" (in Skipp, 1962).

Even across an ocean, Perkins tried to keep him working:

> Let the thing [an unpaid dentist's bill] ride if you like, and it will be fixed up, when you get back, some way. Come back with the novel finished and that amount of money will seem trifling. I enclose herewith some remarks about the *Angel* by Mr. Sinclair Lewis, who recently wrote to congratulate us on publishing it. When they interviewed him about getting the Nobel Prize, he immediately began to talk about your book, and mentioned one or two others at all. We put what he said in an ad (Perkins, 1950).

By early the next year, 1931, Wolfe was "simply living with the book." He wanted to work on it in Europe for at least another six weeks, and then return. "When I get back I want to see you and go to that speakeasy again." Reminiscing about their evenings together drinking, eating and walking, he said, "To me, that is joy; you are a little older and more restrained, but I think you had a good time, too" (in Berg, 1978).

Perkins told Wolfe to keep writing. "My great hope is someday to see you walk in with a manuscript two or three inches thick." By the end of February, Wolfe cabled:

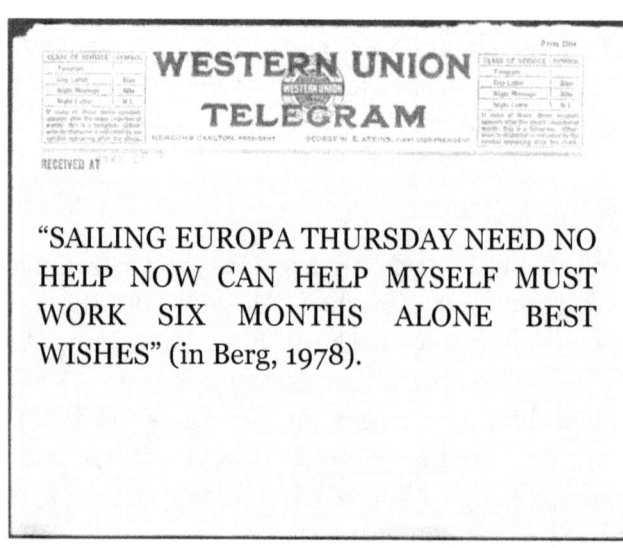

"SAILING EUROPA THURSDAY NEED NO HELP NOW CAN HELP MYSELF MUST WORK SIX MONTHS ALONE BEST WISHES" (in Berg, 1978).

The wandering poet was coming home.

Wolfe got right to work in his new flat in Brooklyn. By August Perkins was anxious to find out what he was writing. "You ought to make every conceivable effort to have your manuscript completely finished by the end of September." Wolfe immediately replied that he would definitely not have a book by this September or any September. He was sensitive to criticism about his lack of production and Perkins had touched a sore spot (Berg, 1978; Skipp, 1962).

By January of the next year, 1932, he was still writing. Perkins told Hemingway, "He has accomplished a great volume of work, and what I have seen of it, not much, is as good as it could be. He keeps getting all upset, and he is so now, and I am to have an evening with him and try to make him think he is some good again. He is good all right." He was still more than two years away from handing Perkins a typescript which was then revised for another year (Skipp, 1962).

Perkins was eager to keep his promising author's name in front of the public, for he knew that in publishing, obscurity breeds anonymity. When he saw that urging Wolfe to finish was not going to speed things up, he picked a long section from the manuscript, "A Portrait of Bascom Hawke," and entered it in the $5,000 prize Long Story Contest of *Scribner's* magazine just before the deadline. Much to the entrant's surprise, he won (Skipp, 1962).

That spring Wolfe was writing to his sister, "Scribner's has been very fine to me of course, but they have begun to push me a little lately. I feel a sense of responsibility and deep obligation to them, and I want to finish the job on time if I can." This meant he wrote from 3-5,000 words a day, much of which was below his usual standard, in Perkins' view (Skipp, 1962).

It became obvious fall publication was impossible. In a July note to the Guggenheim Foundation reporting on his progress, Wolfe said, "I am going ahead daily with my book, or one section of it, which no matter what publisher's announcements and statements say, will be published when I am done writing it and when I think it is fit to be published" (in Skipp, 1962).

Perkins used a carrot as well as a stick. He told Wolfe that if he could get the book together for fall, he would take a half-year sabbatical to drive cross country with him in a Ford. Did not work (Berg, 1978).

He then decided more forceful action was necessary, asking Wolfe to accompany him on a trip to Johns Hopkins for hay fever treatment that he had been postponing. They were together almost constantly on the trip, and Perkins finally figured out what Wolfe had been writing about. He persuaded him to go back and pick up his hero's story where he had left off in *Angel* and go in a straight line (Skipp, 1962).

On the trip back from Hopkins, Wolfe mentioned another story he had written, and Perkins realized there were dozens of stories just waiting to have something done to them. He told Wolfe, "For Heaven's sake, bring it in, and let us publish it." After the usual procrastination, Wolfe turned over 60,000 words of some of his best writing (Berg, 1978).

Perkins ruminated on all Wolfe had told him of his work, and on what he had seen, and mentally fit the puzzle together. As Berg (1978) says, "He realized that they could be made to complete the gigantic manuscript Wolfe was working on. After assembling the pieces in his mind, Perkins called Wolfe and said, "All you have to do is close your hand, and you have your novel." He made Wolfe promise to put it all together based on what direction he had already given him. Wolfe actually delivered as scheduled, and Perkins got right to work (Berg, 1978)

After reading all the new material, Perkins still believed they were getting close to an actual novel. He wrote to a friend, "I'm meditating a plot to get it and him off into the country for a month with me. It will be an agonizing month, though." It never happened (Berg, 1978). He also told Scribner,

> He brought me on Saturday something like 300,000 words of manuscript, considerable sections of which I had seen before. We already had here about 100 or 150,000 words. There's more to be done to fill in, but the book is really almost in existence now...But I really think that his book has half a dozen chapters in it that are beyond anything even in *The Angel;* and it may be a distinctly finer book than that (Berg, 1978).

Perkins dutifully waded through the book-to-be and wrote out a memo with specific revisions. These were not phrased as suggestions, but rather as specifics on how to proceed (Skipp, 1962).

Wolfe mentioned in August that he was finishing up a section he would call "The Hills Beyond Pentland," which surprised Perkins because that was not in their current plan. He wrote to him, "Why don't you give me the section...and let me read it, and so get familiar with that?—Because when we get the book ready for the printer, you will probably want me also to understand it fully, all around. And it is a big book, and not easy to grasp...I wish you would give me that section and let me read it and say nothing about it." Wolfe complied (Skipp, 1962; Berg, 1978).

They were still two years from publication.

Now that some copy was in hand, the work began. Perkins rearranged his schedule so the two met daily, although Perkins usually had to wait for his tardy author. Brooding over his Bernstein problems, Wolfe was drinking more and Perkins sometimes was confronted with a collaborator unable to work at all. Perkins began to get more worried that Wolfe was headed for a breakdown. One day, Perkins stood in the Scribner's hallway and announced, "I think I'll have to take the book away from him" (in Berg, 1978).

Wolfe agreed, feeling he had no other alternative. For six days he sat on his apartment floor with his manuscript. At 11:30 p.m. on December 14, 1933, he arrived late for his appointment and put a big bundle on his editor's desk, wrapped in brown paper, twice tied with string, two feet high. Inside Perkins found more than 3,000 rough draft pages, the first part of *Of Time and River*. The sheets were not numbered. Wolfe told his mother, "God knows a lot of it is still fragmentary and broken up, but at any rate he can now look at it and give me an opinion" (Berg, 1978).

Perkins decided that what they had was two books and he divided it into two cycles, to be published separately. Wolfe recounts, "[Perkins] found that the book did describe two complete and separate cycles...and although the second of the two which became *The Web and the Rock* was by far the more finished, the first cycle, of course, was the one which logically we ought to complete and publish first, and we decided on this course" (in Skipp, 1962).

This first cycle was "a movement which described the period of wandering and hunger in a man's youth," growing out of the idea that "every man is searching for his father." The man, once again, was Eugene Gant, the hero of *Angel*. The second part, "described the period of great certitude, and was dominated by the unity of a single passion," the story of George "Monk" Webber (Berg, 1978).

The manuscript was, by Wolfe's exaggerated count, one million words in length, 12 times the size of an average novel and twice the length of *War and Peace*. Also, as Perkins said, "The book was far from finished. It was in great fragments, and they were not in order...Large parts were missing...It was all disproportioned." Perkins also knew what would happen when Wolfe started filling in gaps (Skipp, 1962).

Their work fell into a pattern. Perkins would take home manuscript sections. Then, after office hours, they would meet at Scribner's or nearby and Wolfe would listen to and argue with

Perkins' advice. By all accounts Perkins did not write much on the manuscript; he would draw a line in a margin by a passage or bend down the corner of a page (Terry, 1953)

Struthers Burt sometimes saw them at a local bar after a session in the office and described the scene.

> Tom would come striding in like a giant who has dined well on human flesh...but always a little cross and pettish with the childish coarseness of a giant. Behind him would be Max, white and utterly exhausted. Max was of average height, but he looked small on those last June nights and sparse like a dry point etching (in Skipp, 1962).

Their arguments continued, Perkins saying that part of an author's duty was to be selective; Wolfe contradicting him with his belief that the author was to illuminate a whole way of life for the reader (Berg, 1978).

Their work was already being discussed in publishing circles. A note appeared in "Books of the Times" which gave credence to the myth: "The man with a legitimate grievance is Maxwell Perkins, the Scribner's editor... They tell stories about Mr. Perkins wrestling with Thomas Wolfe for three days, catch as catch can over the attempted excision of a phrase" (Berg, 1978).

In early 1934, tension was mounting again. Wolfe told a writer-friend, "I went into a slump of awful dejection for two or three weeks after leaving your place [at New Year's]. Was doing little work except cutting and going over the manuscript with Perkins every day. We really got a great deal accomplished, but I was not getting on with my own work at home." A new typist helped Wolfe get back to writing the missing scenes. Yet, in February, when he received a rival publisher's offer of $10,000, he let it go because of his anger at the rival's disparagement of Perkins. By that spring, he let his new typist type all he had that was in manuscript so Perkins could see "the whole work so far as possible." As he wrote to a friend, "I no longer seem to be able to tell what's what myself" (in Skipp, 1962; Berg, 1978).

Wolfe also received an offer to serialize the book in the *American Mercury*, but Perkins suggested he turn it down. He felt the book was too long to serialize, they would have to wait so long, and that Scribner's should keep first crack at it. Wolfe wrote to his mother:

> I think he is right, because he certainly has been the best friend I ever had and has worked for my success and stood by me in the most wonderful and unselfish way. I am convinced that his first and strongest wish has been to see me do a fine piece of work, and that any thought of profit which might come to Scribner's as a result of it has been secondary (Wolfe, 1943).

But after an unusually bitter quarrel in March, he gave Perkins the manuscript to work on by himself (in Skipp, 1962). At the same time Perkins was writing to Rawlings:

> If he will go on for six weeks more at the present rate, the book will be virtually done. I could even now, if I dared, send one-third of it to the printer. But Tom is always threatening to go back to the early part, and if he does that, I do not know what the result will be. We might have to go through the whole struggle over again. It has become an obsession with me now (in Berg, 1978).

The duo was now working seven nights a week. Wolfe would pull a chair up to a corner of Perkins' desk and write out a necessary scene right there. Perkins would read slowly and make his notes. Each slash on a page indicating a cut was followed by Wolfe's eye, followed by a wince. Perkins would say, "I think this section should be omitted." After a long pause, Wolfe would say, "I think it's good." "I think it's good, too, but you have expressed the thing already." "Not the same thing." And so on (Berg, 1978).

One incident stood out. "It was late on a hot night," Perkins reports,

> and we were working at the office. I put my case to him and then sat in silence, reading on in the manuscript...for no less than 15 minutes, but I was aware of Tom's movements—aware at last that he was fixedly looking at one corner of the office. In that corner hung my hat, and overcoat, and down from under the hat, along the coat, hung a sinister rattlesnake skin with seven rattles [a present from underlings]. "Aha!" Wolfe exclaimed, "The portrait of an editor" (in Berg, 1978).

When Perkins sent Wolfe out to write about the death of Gant, a task of 5,000 words, they both agreed, he came back with several thousand words about the old man's doctor. "This is good Tom, but what has it do with the book?" Perkins said. The next night he brought in an equally long passage about the hero's sister. The night after that thousands of extraneous words about Gant's illness, each time agreeing with Perkins that that was not what he was to write. As it turned out, the pages were too good for even Perkins to cut, and Gant's death scene stayed in, "one of the finest passages Wolfe ever wrote," as Berg says (Berg, 1978; Skipp, 1962).

That summer, Perkins turned down a Hemingway vacation to stay in New York and work:

> I cannot leave as long as I can keep Tom going well, as he is doing now. We have over half the book finished, except for a little touching up on another reading. We have got a good system now. We work every evening from 8:30 (or as near as Tom can come to it) until 10:30 or 11, and Tom does actual writing at times, and does it well, where pieces have to be joined up...A couple of nights ago, I told Tom that a whole lot of fine stuff he had in simply ought to come out because it resulted in blurring a very

> important effect. Literally, we sat here for an hour thereafter without saying a word, while Tom glowered and pondered and fidgeted in his chair. Then he said, "Well, then will you take the responsibility?" and I said, "I have simply got to take the responsibility. And what's more," I said, "I will be blamed either way." But he did it, and in the end he knew he was right (Perkins, 1950).

In the beginning of July the book went to the printer. Wolfe felt jubilant and fearful. He wrote to another author, "I feel like a man who has swum upward from some horrible sea-depth where he thought he was last lost and buried forever and come back into the friendly and glorious light of day again" (Skipp, 1962).

Skipp's (1962) analysis of the typescript shows that only three hands actually wrote on the pages: Perkins, Wolfe, and an unidentified feminine hand, which changed the narrative from the first to third person. Most of the significant changes were definitely made in Wolfe's handwriting. One of the styles cuts material

> only with a soft pencil, making it out with irregular and wandering lines, scribbles, and haphazard undulations, sometimes indecisively indicated, but usually applied with very heavy pressure. It bears an unmistakable quality [and is therefore ascribed to Wolfe]...

> Perkins' writing, on the other hand, is neat and precise. The material cut is ordinarily indicated by four clean brackets placed at each corner (if the passage is a number of lines deep, as most often it is) and a straight line drawn from top to bottom through the center of the material. Sometimes instead of a vertical line there is an X with arms pointing towards the corners of the four brackets. Coolness and decisiveness are suggested (Skipp, 1962).

Wolfe's cuts fade out after page 300 and Perkins' hand takes over. Wolfe however continued to mark words and phrases interlinearly, revising. In effect, the two of them cut the "million words" down to 415,000 (Skipp, 1962).

Skipp (1962) concludes:

> Perkins broke eggs to make his omelet, it is difficult to see how he could have done otherwise. Three sections bore to one another but a tangential relation, and to fit them together, unaltered, within conventional covers would have been impossible, so long as publication was controlled by the economics of modern commerce.

Wolfe did work in a vacation trip to the Chicago World's Fair, and when he came back he found his editor was going to send the galleys back to the typesetter without his looking at them. "You can't do it," he said. "The book is not yet finished. I must have six months more on it." In *The Story of a Novel,* Wolfe recorded Perkins' side of the argument: "[He told me that] I was not a perfectionist. I had 20, 30, almost any number of books in me, and the important thing was to get them produced and not to spend the rest of my life perfecting one" (Berg, 1978).

In October 1934 the galleys went to the printer to be set in pages, and in January they received foundry proof. Perkins and Wheelock alone read the galleys and the page proof. Wolfe never could bring himself to proof his set of galleys. Nowell found them on the floor of his apartment just before Wolfe was to sail for Europe. He told her, "That's the reader's set of galleys for my book. I was supposed to read them, but I guess it's too late now." Perkins seemed glad that he was out of the way, since now it really could be published (Skipp, 1962).

Perkins urged Wolfe to drop the foreword he had written to the book, which eventually became *The Story of a Novel.* As for the dedication, Wolfe had been mentally drafting it, and now was working on it with Wheelock's help. Perkins suspected it was to him, and he was right (Berg, 1978). He felt he should tell Wolfe how he really felt:

> Nothing could give me greater pleasure or greater pride as an editor, than that the book of the writer whom I have most greatly admired should be dedicated to me if it were sincerely done.
>
> But you cannot and should not try to change your convictions that I have deformed your book, or at least prevented it from coming to perfection. It is therefore impossible for you sincerely to dedicate it to me and it ought not to be done (Perkins, 1950).

Perkins felt the dedication insincere because he knew how Wolfe felt, but he did not realize how capable Wolfe was of feeling, as Skipp (1962) says, "gratitude and resentment almost simultaneously." The resentment came out eventually; the dedication showed the gratitude:

> To Maxwell Evarts Perkins
>
> A great editor and a brave and honest man, who stuck to the writer of this book through times of bitter hopelessness and doubt and would not let him give in to his own despair, a work to be known as *Of Time and the River* is dedicated with the hope that all of it may be in some way worthy of the loyal devotion and the patient care which a dauntless and unshaken friend has given to each part of it, and without which none of it could have been written (in Berg, 1978).

After publication, many of Perkins' authors concurred with the dedication. Fitzgerald wrote, "I am sure that nothing Tom has said in his dedication could exaggerate the debt that he owes to you—and that stands for all of us who have been privileged to be your authors" (in Berg, 1978).

MANAGER AS MUSE   181

Publication day was March 8, 1935, and Perkins felt he had to write to Wolfe in Europe to let him know of the good reviews. He sent a cable:

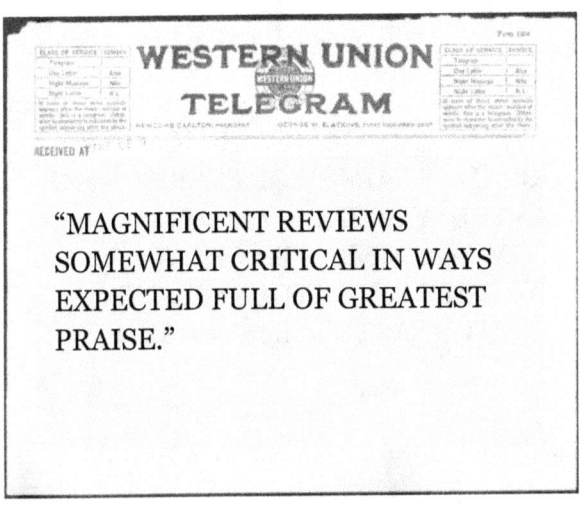

"MAGNIFICENT REVIEWS SOMEWHAT CRITICAL IN WAYS EXPECTED FULL OF GREATEST PRAISE."

Picking up his mail, Wolfe claims he rambled through the streets of Paris in such a reverie that he remembered nothing of the next six days (Berg, 1978).

But naturally, the words "somewhat critical" echoed in Wolfe's mind (Skipp, 1962). He wired back,

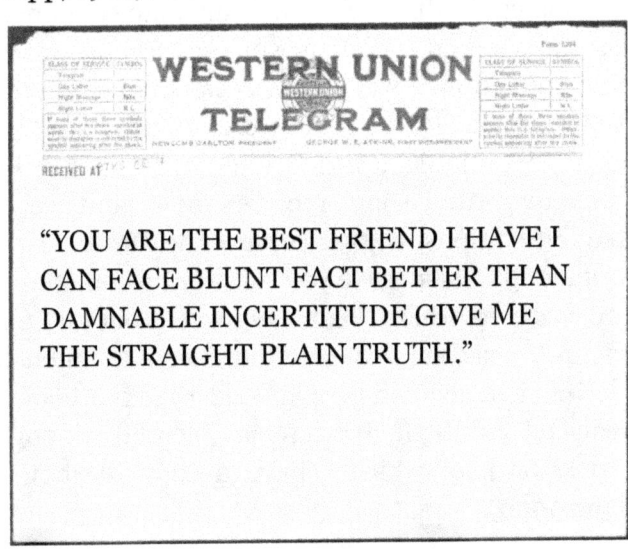

"YOU ARE THE BEST FRIEND I HAVE I CAN FACE BLUNT FACT BETTER THAN DAMNABLE INCERTITUDE GIVE ME THE STRAIGHT PLAIN TRUTH."

Perkins poured it on thicker in the next telegram:

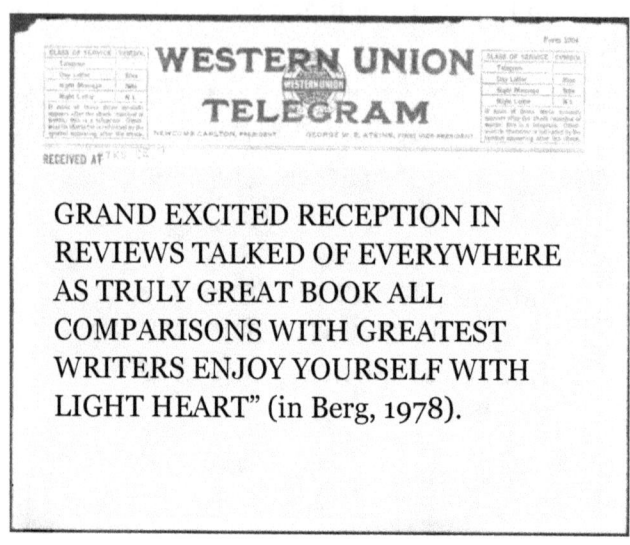

GRAND EXCITED RECEPTION IN REVIEWS TALKED OF EVERYWHERE AS TRULY GREAT BOOK ALL COMPARISONS WITH GREATEST WRITERS ENJOY YOURSELF WITH LIGHT HEART" (in Berg, 1978).

As usual, Perkins followed his wire with a letter:

> Honestly, unless you expected no degree of adverse criticism at all, because of course there was that about too great length and the sort of things we all talked of, I cannot imagine why you should have any restraint upon your happiness in this vacation. If any man could rest on laurels for a bit, the man is you...As for the sale, we cannot yet tell how it will go on, because a large number of copies—some 15, 17,000—were distributed to the stores and it will take a little while for them to sell out. But we are getting some reorders now, and we have printed five editions, 30,000 copies. The *Times, Tribune,* and *Saturday Review* gave you full front pages, and your picture was everywhere. People who went out on Sunday afternoon to teas, etc., ...where there were no publishing people but just regular people, said that the book was excitedly talked about. We have a splendid window [in the bookstore], of which I have a copy to show you (Perkins, 1950).

Along with the good reviews, came an intimation of what was to follow, in *Publisher's Weekly:*

> It is well known that Mr. Wolfe's manuscript assumed mammoth proportions and that he can no more write briefly or economically than an avalanche can check its course...The story goes that Mr. Wolfe was asked to cut the original 900,000 word manuscript in half. He took it home and later returned with 4,000 words cut and 40,000 new words added! So that upon Mr. Perkins alone devolved the responsibility of cutting and arranging the manuscript until it was in shape to be published (in Skipp, 1962).

The book was a success critically and financially. Wolfe came back to the States in July, after being toasted as a hero in Germany, and found that he was a hero at home, too. The book sold more than 40,000 copies in the States and Wolfe had nearly $13,000 to deposit in his first checking account (Skipp, 1962).

What to work on next? Wolfe began thinking of the next work, the second cycle that had been set aside. There was the unfinished *Pentland* book, a draft of something Wolfe called *The Book of the Night,* and lots of short stories. He described one non-autobiographical project Perkins was excited about, but Wolfe didn't know if he could write it. Perkins felt he could and encouraged him. Despite their quarrels, he still wanted to remain close to Perkins and told him of his work, "I will go down deeper in myself than I ever have before. You must try to help me in every way to do this" (in Berg, 1978).

At times Wolfe was still haunted by the incompleteness of his book. Wheelock reports that he was awakened more than once in the middle of the night by phone calls from Wolfe chastising him, "Look at line 37 on page 487 of *Of Time and the River.* Do you see that 'I'? You should have changed that 'I' to 'he.' You betrayed me, and I thought you were my friend!" (in Nowell, 1960).

The Break between Perkins and Wolfe

Because of its importance in their editorial relationship, the break between Wolfe and Perkins will be examined in more detail. This incident, which extended over several years, has been the center of much of the controversy over how much Perkins did for Wolfe and also raises this all-important question for those who manage creative people: When have you gone too far?

Skipp (1962) points out that those who were close to the two noted signs of friction while they were still working on *River*. "Editor and author were by no means united in their views of how the manuscript was to be cut and shaped. Their disagreements were frequent, and, on Wolfe's part at least, noisy. There was often high emotional tension between the two."

This was noted within the publishing world. Basso first reported in the *New Republic* in June 1936, "when Max Perkins cut some 50,000 words from *Of Time and the River* at one sitting, Wolfe was aghast. ' This,' he shouted, banging his fists on the table, 'is the greatest crime since Judas betrayed Christ!'" Those who knew Wolfe knew that he meant it with no hyperbole.

At this time Scribner's still handled Wolfe's money, which was wise given his appetites and temperament. His average yearly earnings from 1928 to 1938 were only about $4,000. After publication of *River,* when he was enjoying some success, Wolfe wanted the chance to control his own money. He and Perkins quarreled over something, not now known. Perkins referred to it as "a big row with Tom" in a letter to Wheelock. As a result, Wolfe withdrew all his cash at the end of 1935, almost $13,000, and opened a bank account, his first step toward independence. This was the first intimation that Wolfe was becoming preoccupied with the financial side of his relationship with Scribner's (Skipp, 1962).

During that whole year, Perkins was wise enough to note that Wolfe was testing their friendship and looking for reasons to quarrel: "I don't mean that Tom was deliberately and consciously inventing reasons for leaving us, but the underlying reasons were working so strongly in him and yet were not consciously acknowledged, that he thought the pretexts were the true reasons" (in Berg, 1978).

The first specific argument concerned money. *The Story of a Novel* was set in print and ready to be published in April 1936. Close to publication date, as usual, Perkins and Wolfe discussed the contract. Because the book would be so much smaller than a normal trade book, the price would have to be lower and Scribner's would have a harder time covering its costs. Perkins offered a reduced royalty on the first printing and Wolfe agreed to go from 15% to 10% for the first 3,000 copies. Just before publication date, however, Wolfe found out that the price on the book would be $1.50, not $1.25 as he had believed. This made him furious. He was receiving a lower royalty, but Scribner's was charging a higher price. When he met Perkins to discuss this, Wolfe went into one of his ugly, name-calling tirades, following up with a note of apology the next morning (Berg, 1978).

Wolfe began to see his editor-friend as a crafty fox who had revealed that he was, in Wolfe's suspicious words, "playing with two sets of counters." He had accepted the lower terms because Perkins had told him that Scribner's would not profit but they felt it was worth publishing anyway (Skipp, 1962). "To prove that he had not been taken advantage of," says Berg (1978), "Wolfe [thought Perkins should restore] his former royalty." Wolfe wrote:

> If you make use of a business advantage in this way, don't you think I would be justified in making use of a business advantage, too, if one came my way: Or do you think it works only one way?...You cannot command the loyalty and devotion of someone on the one hand and then take a business advantage on the other (in Berg, 1978).

One week before publication, Perkins (1950) wrote to him:

> I am giving direction to reckon your royalties on *The Story of a Novel* at 15% from the start. The difference in what you will receive, if 3,000 copies are sold, between the ten and 15% royalty, will be $225.00. We certainly do not think that we should withhold that sum of money if it is going to cause so much resentment and so much loss of time and disquiet for all of us.
>
> I would rather simply agree to do this and say nothing further, but I should not have the right to do it without telling you that the terms, as proposed, on the $1.50 price are just, and that if the matter were to be looked upon merely as business we should not be justified as business men in making this concession...

Wolfe was contrite upon receiving Perkins' letter: "Life is too short to quarrel this way with a friend over something that matters so little... All the damn contracts in the world didn't mean as much to me as your friendship." He said he would abide by the original terms, ending with, "I am now started on another book. I need your friendship and support more than I ever did, so please forget the worst mistakes I have made in the past and let's see if I can't do somewhat better in the future" (Skipp, 1962; Berg, 1978).

Just as this argument quieted down came the biggest blow to the Perkins-Wolfe friendship, and it came from the outside. Bernard DeVoto's review of *The Story of a Novel*, "Genius Is Not Enough," was actually an excuse for an attack on Wolfe's writing. Extensive excerpts are quoted here because it is the pivotal point around which Wolfe's final break with Scribner's turned:

> Well, *The Story of a Novel* puts an end to speculation and supplies some unexpected but very welcome light. The most flagrant evidence of his incompleteness is the fact that, so far, one indispensable part of the artist has

existed not in Mr. Wolfe but in Max Perkins. Such organizing faculty and such critical intelligence as have been applied to the book have come not from inside the artist, but from the office of Charles Scribner's Sons. For five years the artist pours out words "like burning lava from a volcano,"—with little or no idea what their purpose is, which book they belong in, what the relation of part to part is, what is organic and what irrelevant, or what emphasis or coloration in the completed work of art being served by the job at hand. Then Mr. Perkins decides these questions—from without and by a process to which rumor applied the word "assembly." But works of art cannot be assembled like a carburetor—they must be grown like a plant, or in Mr. Wolfe's favorite simile, like an embryo. The artist writes 100,000 words about a train: Mr. Perkins decides the train is worth only 5,000 words. But such a decision as this is not properly within Mr. Perkins' power; it must be made by the highly conscious self-criticism of the artist...

Worse still, the artist goes on writing till Mr. Perkins tells him that the novel is finished. But the end of the novel is properly dictated by the internal pressures, osmosis, metabolism—what you will—of the novel itself, of which only the novelist can have a firsthand knowledge...

However useful genius may be in the writing of novels, it is not enough in itself—it never has been enough, in any art, and it never will be. At the very least it must be supported by an ability to impart shape to the material, simple competence in the use of tools.

Until Mr. Wolfe develops more craftsmanship, he will not be the important novelist he is now widely accepted as being. In order to be a great novelist he must also mature his emotions till he can see more profoundly into character than he now does, and he must learn to put a corset on his prose...His own smithy is the only possible place for these developments. They cannot occur in the office of any editor whom he will ever know (in Berg, 1978; DeVoto, 1936; Skipp, 1962).

At first Wolfe was angry, but, in Skipp's (1962) view at least, it did not "throw him off balance. Although Wolfe felt that the sum of what DeVoto said was a lie, he admitted that there was truth in it." Nor did Wolfe apparently feel any lessening of affection for Perkins or any reluctance to go on accepting his judgment, at first.

However, within a month, his letters were hinting that the time had come to leave Scribner's (Skipp, 1962). Berg (1978) interprets Wolfe's feelings this way:

> In a single blow DeVoto had destroyed Wolfe's pleasure of accomplishment. It was one thing to give Perkins his due. It was quite another for the critic to turn his gesture against him, to make his books seem the product of a "factory." Wolfe lashed out against DeVoto to anyone who would listen, but on a deeper level the rage was probably directed at Max. The fact that Perkins, far from seeking this public credit, had yearned to elude him made no difference to Tom when his emotions were running. Max had taught him, by implication, that the editor remains "in the background." Now Max, thanks to DeVoto, was forever to be out front. It was something Tom could definitely not abide and no one knew this sooner or more surely than Max.

His initial feelings were that DeVoto's article was a challenge and that he should now take up Perkins' tossed gauntlet and write his "objective" book. His fury went into his writing for a while. But by the summer of 1936 he was so inflamed as to tell everyone that he was equal "to all the DeVotos in the world" (Berg, 1978).

At the same time, Perkins found out through Nowell that Wolfe was writing about a publishing company. Perkins knew immediately his material would come not only from his firsthand experience with Scribner's, but from all the intimate details Perkins had told him in their evenings of camaraderie. Perkins read the story in question, "No More Rivers," in Nowell's presence. She reports, "At first he sat bolt upright at his desk, with unusually pink cheeks and blazing eyes, and refused to discuss the story." Then he took her for a drink and began to talk a little bit. "Perkins felt like kicking himself. 'I should have known better,' he admitted...'but I've told Tom all kinds of highly confidential things about the firm and about the people there.'" He did not object to what Wolfe would write about Perkins, but what he would write about what Perkins had told him about everyone else (Skipp, 1962; Berg, 1978).

As if these bones of contention were not enough, during that summer Wolfe was being bothered by two lawsuits which made him question Scribner's motives. He also felt Scribner's might refuse to publish what he was working on, coming as close as it did to the truth (Skipp, 1962).

Wolfe held Perkins accountable for the first lawsuit, by his former agent Boyd, suing for royalties on *River*. He told his editor that it came about because "We were foolish, benevolent, soft hearted, weak—call it what you like." Wolfe saw it as Perkins' failure to demand that Boyd sign a written release as soon as she and Wolfe began to quarrel. Perkins' failure to do this, Wolfe felt, encouraged Boyd to pursue her suit. He reproached Perkins with this many times (Skipp, 1962).

Wolfe also became furious with Scribner's when a former landlady of his sued him for libel because she felt she and her family were misrepresented in one of his stories. Scribner's advised settling out of court. He wrote to Perkins of both these entanglements, "The editorial relationship between us...has now lost its initial substance. It has become a myth—and what is worse than that an untrue myth" (in Madison, 1966).

Scribner's agreed to be co-defendant in the suit, although their standard contract with Wolfe for the stories in *From Death to Morning* had the author guaranteeing that the book libeled no one and that he would hold the publisher harmless. They also agreed to pay half of the costs. Scribner's retained an "enormously reputable and enormously expensive," as Skipp (1962) said, law firm, which was as conservative as Perkins and Scribner, but not Wolfe.

All the conservatives advised the young writer to settle now. They knew that his work was suffering, as Perkins remembered later:

> Tom simply could not take it. It was for that reason that we settled the lawsuit, although we never did tell him so. He was so tormented that he could do nothing but drink and brood. It was absolutely necessary to get the thing out of the way and this was done only with his apparent satisfactory agreement. But afterward he did think we had let him down (in Berg, 1978).

They settled with the landlord for $3,000 and there were $2,000 more in legal fees. Although the terms of his contract would have held Wolfe liable to pay the entire expense, Scribner's offered to pay half (Berg, 1978).

By November of that year, Wolfe finalized a letter he had drafted a few times and mailed it to Perkins:

> I think you should now write me a letter in which you explicitly state the nature of my relationship with Charles Scribner's Sons. I think you ought to say that I have faithfully and honorably discharged all obligations..., whether financial, personal, or contractual, and that no further agreement or obligation of any sort exists between us.

I also think that it is unfair that a man without income, with little money and with no economic security against the future, who has time and again in the past refused offers and proposals that would have brought him comfort and security, should now, at a time when his reputation has been obscured, and when there are no offers and little market for his work, be compelled to this last and sorrowful exercise of his fruitless devotion (in Berg, 1978).

Perkins received this letter just before the monthly board meeting, and so sent a handwritten note which said:

I never knew a soul with whom I felt I was in such fundamentally complete agreement as you. What's more...I know you would not ever do an insincere thing, or anything you did not think was right. I don't fully understand your letter but I'll answer it as best I can. You must surely know, though, that any publisher would leap at the chance to publish you.

Always yours,

You have with us at present a balance of over $2,000, all but about $500 of which is overdue (Perkins, 1950).

The next day he was able to write a complete response on his personal letterhead (Berg, 1978):

With this is a more formal letter which I hope is what you want. This is to say that on my part there has been no "severance." I can't express certain kinds of feelings very comfortably, but you must realize what my feelings are toward you. Ever since *Look Homeward, Angel* your work has been the foremost interest in my life and I have never doubted for your future on any grounds except, at times, on those of your being able to control the vast mass of material you have accumulated and have to form into books. You seem to think I have tried to control you. I only did that when you asked my help and then I did the best I could. It all seems very confusing to me but, whatever the result, I hope you don't mean it will keep us from seeing each other, or that you won't come to our house (Perkins, 1950).

The formal letter stated:

> You have faithfully and honorably discharged all obligations to us and no further agreement of any sort exists between us with respect to the future. Our relations are simply those of a publisher who profoundly admires the work of an author and takes great pride in publishing whatever he may of that author's writings. They are not such as to give any sort of rights, or anything approaching that, over the author's future work. Contrary to custom, we have not even an option which would give us the privilege of seeing first any new manuscripts (Perkins, 1950).

Within two days, Scribner's sent the money on to Wolfe, with a cover letter from Perkins saying, "I wish I could see you, but I don't want to force myself on you" (in Berg, 1978).

In fact, Wolfe came to the Perkins' home for Christmas and they all talked pleasantly about his upcoming trip to New Orleans. He did not mention a long personal letter that he had written ten days before, outlining his reasons for wanting to break away completely, nor a supplementary "business" letter he had written only two days before. He carried both these with him for weeks not knowing whether he should send them. The business letter was never mailed, but at the turn of the year he was deciding to send the personal letter (Berg, 1978).

This letter was, to say the least, impassioned. About DeVoto's attack he said that the critic had tried to twist his meaning in *The Story of a Novel*. He acknowledged Perkins' "spiritual" help, but said that he had found his own direction and was certain of it (Skipp, 1962).

Yet another lawsuit was vexing Wolfe while he was in New Orleans. It concerned a young man who had offered to sell some of Wolfe's manuscripts and then had refused to give them or the proceeds back to Wolfe. Once again, Scribner's said settle and Wolfe said no. In another letter which was mailed with his personal letter, Wolfe said to Perkins: "Are you—the man I trusted and reverenced above all else in the world—trying, for some mad reason I cannot even guess, to destroy me?" (in Berg, 1978).

Wolfe agreed that he and Perkins were, in a strange way, in "complete and fundamental agreement...Where there ever two men since time began who were as completely different as you and I? Have you ever known two other people who were, in almost every respect and temperament, thinking, feeling and acting as far apart?" He felt Perkins was the conservative while he was the Revolutionary, although he was not sure if these labels "got it right" (Berg, 1978).

Wolfe had conceived of his greatest work yet, but was afraid to mention it to Perkins. He felt there was already a break, and, if Perkins disagreed,

> tell me what there is in the life around us on which we both agree: We don't agree in politics, we don't agree on economics, we are in entire disagreement on the present system of life around us, the way people live, and the changes that should be made...I am now going write as I plan, and this time, no one is going to cut me unless I want them to...Restrain my adjectives, by all means, discipline my adverbs, moderate the technical extravagance of my incondite exuberance, but don't derail the train, don't take the Pacific Ltd. and switch it down the siding toward Hogwart Junction...

> [To continue to write for Scribner's would mean submitting] to the most rigid censorship, a censorship which would delete from all my writings any episode, any scene, any character, any reference that might seem to have any connection, however remote, with the house of Charles Scribner's Sons and its sisters and its cousins and its aunts (in Berg, 1978).

Perkins had told Wolfe that he was "always with the man of talent," and rather than restrict the author, he would resign from Scribner's (Berg, 1978). To this Wolfe wrote,

> Well, don't worry. You'll never have to...Your executive and editorial functions are so specialized and valuable that they could not be substituted by any other person on earth. They could not be done without by the business that employs them. It would be like having a house with the lights turned out...I won't be there to be resigned about (in Berg, 1978).

To Wolfe's impassioned ramblings, Perkins replied in mid-January 1937:

> My belief is that the one important, supreme object is to advance your work. Anything in furtherance of that is good and anything that impedes it is bad...

> There were places in your letter that made me angry, but it was a fine letter, a fine writer's statement of his beliefs, as fine as any I ever saw, and though I have vanities enough, as many as most, it gave me great pleasure, too—that which comes from hearing brave and sincere beliefs uttered with sincerity and nobility (Perkins, 1950).

He wrote again to Wolfe two days later (Berg, 1978):

> Since I have always thought that there could be nothing so important as a book can be, and some are, I could not

help but think as you do. But there are limitations of time, of space, and of human laws which cannot be treated as if they did not exist...I have always held to that position and have sometimes seen books hurt thereby, but at least as often helped. "The book belongs to the author"...

You were never overruled. Do you think you are clay to be molded! I never saw anyone less malleable. And as for publishing what you like or being prevented from it, apart from the limitations of space, you have not been, intentionally...

Tom, you ought not to say some of the things you do— that I find your sufferings amusing and don't take them seriously. I know something of them. I do try to turn your mind from them and to arouse your humor...Have you seen me amused by other people's sufferings. You know that was unjust.

Then comes the question of your writing about the people here. I don't want to discuss it, because I agree that you have the same right to make use of them as of anyone else in the same way...But when I spoke of resigning after we publish...I did not mean I would be asked or wanted to resign...And it's up to you to write as you think you should. Your plan outlined seems to me a splendid one, too. I hope you will get on with it now (Perkins, 1950).

Perkins' letter calmed Wolfe down enough that he delayed his departure from Scribner's, although in his own mind he had already separated from them (Berg, 1978).

A letter fragment, probably written to his lawyer at this time reads:

> I know I am alone now...As for Mr. Perkins—he is the great editor [of this generation]. I revered and honored him also as the great man, the great friend, the greatest character I had ever known...As for the rest—he is an honest but a timid man. He is not a man for danger—I expect no help from...[Unfinished] (in Berg, 1978).

As for Perkins, he kept Wolfe's letter in his desk and Wheelock says that he would see his fellow editor pull it out at various times during the day and re-read it trying to make sense of the whole affair. "That particular letter very nearly killed Max. But he never struck back. Tom Wolfe was the ultimate editorial challenge, part of which meant dealing with his personal temperament," Wheelock said (in Berg, 1978).

Marcia Davenport, another Perkins author, met Wolfe aboard ship when he was going through his mental "break." She could not recall later exactly what he had said to her, but the gist of it was "his intention to prove that he was not, as he claimed the literary world believed, the creature of Max Perkins." As Berg (1978) describes the scene,

> "I'm going to show them I can write my books without Max. I'm going to leave Max and get another editor. I'm going to leave Scribner's," he told Mrs. Davenport.
>
> "How about the dedication in your last book?" she asked, "Are you that much of a hypocrite?" Wolfe ignored the remark and went on to complain that Perkins had kept out of the book some of the best things he had ever written. Over and over he repeated his need to leave Scribner's, until Marcia Davenport let him have it.
>
> "I think you're a rat," she said. "You're ungrateful and treacherous. That dedication was disgusting. It didn't mean devotion to Max, it was just spilling yourself. You have no devotion and no loyalty either. Where would you be without Max and Scribner's too? You can't face the

truth." Months later, those accusations were still festering in Wolfe's mind.

> **Two sample satirical titles...**
>
> ...of the type Wolfe used to write when trying to formulate ideas were found in his notebooks:
>
> A modest pamphlet Tending to prove that writers (and all others of their Ilk) Shall Be Allowed to Live and if the Goddamned Sons of bitches Go Not Too Hardly at the Task to Earn a Living and if It Be Not Too Much to Suppose to Be Allowed To Draw Their Breath Occasionally Without Aging, Labor, Horror, Death, Damnation, and Attendant Abomination In This Home of Free People and Free Speech, The U. S. of America...

> A Modest Commercial Proposal—Tending to Prove That Authors Are Members of the Human Race and That If They Are Properly Dealt With They Are As Tractable As Most Other People and That the Publishing Profession Although It Is As Well-Known a Beneficent and Philanthropic Enterprise Established As An Avocation by Gentlemen of Culture and Sporting Tastes Where Fathers and Kinsmen Made Their Money Out of Society Else May Still Derive Some Profit Occasionally If the Matter Be Shrewdly Dealt with Out of the Author, The Body, Bones, Brains, Sweat, Etc., of a Living Man—(in Skipp, 1962).

Although both felt their friendship had been wounded—though not killed—by the exchange of letters, Wolfe continued to visit the Perkins' home almost every day. He wrote at this time to Basso: "Yes, Max Perkins and I are all right. I think we always were, for that matter. Periodically, I go out and indulge in a 60-

round, knock down and drag out battle with myself but I think Max understands that." He held to the dictum he had read somewhere that "no writer has ever yet been known to hang himself as long as he had another chapter left" (Berg, 1978).

Wolfe was trying to draft a letter to send to other publishers, unskilled as he was in the ways of the publishing world. He never sent the letter but became obsessed with the idea of leaving Scribner's so that he talked of nothing else. Finally, in exasperation, Perkins told him one night, "All right then, if you must leave Scribner's, go ahead and <u>leave,</u> but for heaven's sake, don't talk about it anymore!" (in Berg, 1978; Nowell, 1956).

By the end of 1937, Wolfe was ready to sign with Harper's (Berg, 1978). Perkins saw the break as inevitable. He wrote to Rawlings, "I can easily imagine a biography of Tom written 20 years from now that would ascribe this action to his instinctive... determination to free all his bonds and stand up alone." Later he wrote to Wolfe, "I drink a lonely glass of ale every night in Manny Wolf's while waiting for the paper...We really had a mighty good Christmas, but we missed you" (in Berg, 1978).

Chard Powers Smith (1962) reports that after Wolfe was finally at Harper's Perkins would tell Wolfe stories he hadn't told before.

> How Tom would call him up any time of the night—perhaps at the office, where Max liked to work in the quiet of the evening, perhaps at his Turtle Bay house, sometimes all the way out at [Connecticut]—and implore him to meet him somewhere. And gentle Max would follow him around all night while Tom got murderous and suicidal drunk...Max told me a story of being in a small restaurant with Tom, who was behaving himself, sitting quietly with his drink at a table near the bar. Suddenly the horror of life so overcame him that he stood

up, stepped to the bar, picked up the cash register and threw it out into the room.

Smith's (1962) impression from Perkins was that the main reason for the break was that Wolfe had reached the point in his one long autobiographical novel where he would have to write about Scribner's and he did not want to "hand in his copy to his victims." The irony, of course, was that Perkins was Wolfe's literary executor at the time of his death, and had the job of editing this same copy for publication. Smith says the editor deleted all the Scribner's characters except Foxhall Edwards, himself, whom he left intact.

Right after Christmas 1937, when Wolfe was working with his new editor, Aswell at Harpers, he had to ask Perkins for help once again. The trial involving the young man who had been peddling Wolfe manuscripts was being held, and Wolfe asked Perkins to testify, "not only for personal or friendly reasons, but just because it's taking a stand in favor of the human race" (in Berg, 1978). They met in the Chelsea Hotel lobby in early February to discuss the details of the case, and found that they could still be cordial and friendly.

A week later Perkins went to Jersey City for the trial. Nowell reports that Wolfe was visibly moved by watching his old friend take the stand in his defense because, for the first time in public, Perkins was wearing a hearing aid. Perkins knew how important it was for him to hear every detail, although he had constantly resisted wearing one before (Berg, 1978).

Perkins wrote to Fitzgerald during the emotional turmoil with Wolfe: "Tom was a kind of great adventure, but all the dreadful imperfections about him took much of the satisfaction out of it. I think at bottom Tom has an idea now that he will go it alone, doing his own work, and if he could manage that, it would be the one and only way in which he could really do what he should" (in

Skipp, 1962). At this same time, spring 1938, Wolfe was writing in his notebooks:

- The Cleavage with Fox
- Women
- Economics
- Politics
- ...the structure of the world (in Skipp, 1967-8).

This is the only place that "women" is included as any part of the reason for the break, Skipp (1967-8) notes, which raises a question about the other causes Wolfe listed. Were they, too, pretexts?

In all his letters to friends and writers, Perkins explained that it was in Wolfe's best interest to move on. "Hemingway, for one," reports Berg (1978), "thought Perkins wrote 'very chic-ly' about it all, while Wolfe had acted like an enormous baby. Ernest wondered why the man could not just write, then sneered that it must be very difficult to be a genius."

At a social evening months later, Perkins said that Wolfe had to leave to advance his work. His loyal author Davenport protested, "Oh, no! He needed you as much as I do. I couldn't write a book without you." "If that were true," Perkins said, "You would not be worth the work that has gone into you" (in Berg, 1978).

Skipp (1962) points out the ethical distinction that Perkins made in his disagreement with Wolfe over using Scribner's characters in his next book. "The editor had attempted to erect a fence between what Wolfe knew of Scribner's from his direct experience there, and what he knew as a result of Perkins' confidential disclosure. Wolfe's creative drive, his creative method itself, rolled right over it."

As to the differences in social philosophy between the two, Skipp (1962) finds that the typescript of Of Time and the River does have material "obviously intended to dramatize inequities in the

American social order." This was cut out by Perkins' hand, but for literary reasons, as he himself says, and the text bears this out.

Another actor in the drama who was privy to both sides was Wolfe's last editor, Aswell. In refuting Burt's claim that Wolfe "killed" Perkins, Aswell (1941) reports:

> From each I heard the story of the break between them and all the circumstances that led up to it...I can say with measured judgment that there was no betrayal in it. Deep feelings were aroused in both men, yes.—but there was no betrayal. Max talked about it a great deal, going back over the events and fitting the pieces together to see how cause led to effect, and he always came up with the conclusion that what happened had been inevitable.

But the best statement of the feeling between the two men to the end was made by Wolfe himself, in literally his deathbed writings, a quick note to Perkins that could be, ironically, the most concise paragraph he ever wrote:

> Whatever happens—I had this "hunch" and wanted to write you and tell you, no matter what happens or has happened, I shall always think of you and feel about you the way it was that Fourth of July day three years ago when you met me at the boat, and we went out on the cafe on the river and had a drink and later went on top of the tall building. And all the strangeness and the glory of and the power of life and of the city was below (Perkins, 1950).

Posthumous Works

Although *Of Time and the River* was the last book that Perkins and Wolfe worked on together, the editor's influence as literary executor shows so strongly in all his published writings that it is worth considering here.

Wolfe signed with Harper's at Christmas of 1937 to work with Aswell. One of his first acts was to immortalize Perkins in fiction. He created a new character, The Fox, otherwise known as Foxhall Edwards. He wanted to conclude his book with a recapitulation of his own career, ending with an open letter entitled, "A Farewell to the Fox." He told Nowell that this section "would be a kind of impassioned summing up of the whole book, of everything that has gone before, and a final statement of what is now" (in Berg, 1978).

The contract Wolfe signed with Harper's specifically stated that "no changes, additions, or alterations in the title or text" of the work would be made without Wolfe's written consent. Aswell was so happy to sign Wolfe that he offered him a $10,000 advance and one month later, Wolfe signed on the dotted line (Halberstadt, 1981).

By May of the next year Wolfe told his new editor that he was at the "same state of articulation as with *Of Time and the River* in December of 1933 [when Perkins saw the entire manuscript for the first time]...What he saw, of course, was only a kind of enormous skeleton but at any rate he was able to get some kind of articulate idea of the whole." He warned Aswell that what he was working on would be a physically bigger book than *River* (Berg, 1978). Wolfe claimed that he turned over to Aswell two million words, but the actual count was closer to one million (Cowley, 1957).

Wolfe then headed out for a long journey to the West that was eventually to cost him his life. In Vancouver he was riding on a ferry in a cold night and shared a bottle of whiskey with a "poor wretch," as he called him afterwards. It is not known if he contracted tuberculosis from this, or opened up previous lesions on his lungs. The infection spread to his brain, and after being diagnosed and treated at a sanitarium in Washington state, he was brought to Johns Hopkins on a long train ride across the country with his sister. When they operated they found that his brain was filled with tubercles and that his case was hopeless. He died soon after, in the fall of 1938, just before his 38th birthday. Perkins and Aswell were at the hospital in his last days, although Perkins did not see Wolfe for fear it would upset him (Berg, 1978).

Perkins and his wife attended the funeral in Asheville. He was an honorary pallbearer, but stood apart from the rest, alone by the trees, in the background. After it was over they took a taxi to drive along Wolfe's mountains that ringed the town, and Perkins realized what an effect they had had on the writer. He wrote years later: "A boy of Wolfe's imagination, imprisoned there, could think that what was beyond was all wonderful" (in Berg, 1978).

Despite their arguments, Wolfe had not changed his will and Perkins was now his literary executor. Fitzgerald saw the irony in this and told his editor that he was now more in control of Wolfe's future than when he had been alive (Berg, 1978).

The estate included the rough draft of the novel under contract to Harpers, in their safe. Perkins' job was to see that it was published along with other work left behind. He approached these crates of manuscript as though Wolfe were still his author. He reviewed the material, itemized each piece, and pulled out pages to be sold as magazine articles (Berg, 1978).

One of the clauses in Wolfe's contract said that he would give Harper's a manuscript that would not exceed 750,000 words, but the crates contained one million words. Aswell and Perkins determined that this meant they could cut at least 250,000 words (Halberstadt, 1981).

The first task, however, was what to do with the journal Wolfe had written on his trip. It was 10,000 words, mostly sentence fragments, merely the raw stuff of a larger work. After they were typed and Perkins re-read them, he suggested publishing the notes as they were, because no change could be made without the author's approval. Only those corrections which may have reasonably been made by Wolfe were included. The diary appeared in the Summer 1939 issue of the *Virginia Quarterly Review,* complete with incomplete sentences, uneven punctuation, etc. under the name, "A Western Journey" (Berg, 1978).

Perkins made notes on the manuscript and then Aswell set to work putting it together. He found that the "wonderful thing about the manuscript...Was that once the extraneous matter was removed,...the parts that remained fell into place and fitted together like the pieces of a jigsaw puzzle" (in Berg, 1978).

Perkins' first known comment on reading the section on "The Fox" was to Aswell: "That man he called the Fox—I don't think Tom got him quite right" (Cowley, 1944). But a few days later he said: "That man Tom calls The Fox—I took the passage home to show my wife and daughters, and they think he did get him right." He did not allow Aswell to change or take out any of the Fox passages (Berg, 1978).

However, the fact that he would now be public once again bothered Perkins. "I just hate to be written about on any account," he told Fitzgerald. "And it seemed odd that with all the designs he had upon Scribner's the only part that he wrote that fits into the book—and it's pretty long—should be about me" (in Berg, 1978).

Naturally, the publication of two books without Perkins' help as editor, raises the question of how they compare with what the two did work on together. Holman (1960) says,

> The sometimes violent midwifery of Perkins may have been essential to getting anything publishable from the laboring author. On the other hand, when one examines the first 300 pages of *The Web and the Rock* and recalls that it is Wolfe's own work done without editorial assistance or thinks of the power and directness of the

first two [sections] of *You Can't Go Home Again,* it is difficult not to wish that Wolfe had been free to try.

As Aswell worked on the manuscript, he realized what Perkins had come to know. That Wolfe didn't really write books. Instead, "Tom really wrote only one book, and that runs to some 4,000 printed pages comprising the total of his works" (in Skipp, 1962).

Wolfe has left behind the best record of his friendship with Perkins in his novels. The Fox is always gentle, patient, and kind and all his effort is devoted to helping others. He is also fatally resigned, that there is "no new thing under the sun." Excerpts from his letter to the Fox show the ambivalent feelings Wolfe held toward his editor-friend all his life:

> You never had a doubt that I would finish...The only doubt was mine, enhanced, tormented by my own fatigue and desperation, and by the clacking of the feeble and malicious little tongues which, knowing nothing, whispered that I would never make an end again because I could not begin...

> Dear Fox, old friend, thus we have come to an end of the road that we were to go together. My tale is finished—and so farewell...For I was lost and was looking for someone older and wiser to show me the way, and I found you, and you took the place of my father, who had died. The road now leads off in a direction contrary to your intent (Wolfe, 1940).

V

Conclusions

Application of Principles

The purpose behind my research into these fascinating characters in early 20th century American literature was to determine how Maxwell Perkins motivated his three most famous authors to create great work. So how do Perkins' management style and techniques compare and contrast with Fayol's guidelines?

Equity:

The editor inspired great devotion and loyalty, accepted responsibility and was considered to be fair.

Descriptions of Perkins' work with all of his authors mention his tremendous fairness and kindness. Perkins took full responsibility for his writers and their work. Indeed his problems with Wolfe may have stemmed from his taking on too much responsibility, stepping over the boundary from editor to co-author. Perkins' work was also characterized by "fair play," along with "forcefulness and sternness" at times. His firmness usually took the form of friendly persuasion, entreaties to the writer to keep writing.

Discipline:
Perkins was not a strong taskmaster but could be firm, inspiring respect in his authors and helping them with their self-control.

In the area of discipline, Perkins once again followed Fayol's principles, although he was never known as a strong disciplinarian. Rather, his discipline was what Fayol called "organized self-control." His authors' obedience took the form of following Perkins' suggestions regarding both their work and their careers, with little if any trace of fear. The only exception to Fayol's sub-principle that discipline must be based on respect, not fear, is Wolfe's protestation that he was afraid to show Perkins his next work because of his fear that Perkins would disregard its importance. In general, his relationships with Wolfe and all his authors were based on tremendous respect.

Remuneration of Personnel:
Personal involvement became very important and the mode of payment depended on the individual's needs.

This area is of great importance to all managers. In fact, the sub-principle which relates most directly to Perkins' dealings with authors is Fayol's belief that the managers should become involved in the workers' private lives—up to a point. Perkins was personal friends with all three writers, took an interest in their lives, spent time with them and their families socially, and handled personal duties for each of them. Perkins' critics have argued that his biggest mistake was taking too much of an interest in Wolfe as a person, treating him as a surrogate son. Even Wolfe has given this as a cause for their famous break, "that the editor and the friend got too close" (Wolfe, 1956).

Fayol did not draw a definite line that the manager should not cross, feeling that he was only setting down guidelines and that the degree of personal involvement would vary with each worker and circumstance. Perkins' involvement with his writers was intrinsic to their success, but when he went too far with Wolfe it led to bad feelings on all sides and the eventual loss of Wolfe to Scribner's. What the dividing line was, what was "too far," and when Perkins should have pulled back is difficult to determine.

Fayol's sub-principle of remuneration being based on "the will of the company and the value of the employee," relates directly to Perkins' manner of financially rewarding his authors. To him the writer's value was not measured in terms of the sale of the next book, but in the long-range benefits of their careers to the company and the authors. He was willing to have Scribner's pay for the long, fallow periods of writers' lives as well as reap the benefits of their lucrative efforts.

The method of payment that Perkins used for each author varied slightly, although all were paid by "job rates," which are defined in Fayol's terms as "payment made turning upon the execution of a definite job set in advance and independent of the length of the job" (Dyer and Dyer, 1969). Fitzgerald survived on his personal and professional advances against future work. With Hemingway, Perkins volunteered to make this payment regular, in the form of an annual salary, but Hemingway declined because he knew he could never write on demand. His earnings were mostly in royalties since his books did so much better during his lifetime than Fitzgerald's did during his. In Wolfe's case, Perkins tried to find many different ways for him to earn a living from writing, including grants and fellowships, sales of segments of his books as stories, as well as the earnings from his books and some advances.

For the most part, Perkins' managerial behavior in the area of remuneration was based on standard rates of exchange in the industry, although many times he knew he was paying an author less—and in some cases more—than could be earned elsewhere. For example, Fitzgerald always earned more from his short stories, but Perkins compensated for this with large advances to keep him writing novels. He knew Hemingway could earn more for articles than *Scribner's* magazine would pay him, but he kept Hemingway in the fold with advances and promises of publisher loyalty. Wolfe's value was difficult to determine, although he felt it had to be at least $10,000 since that was what another publisher had offered. Perkins kept him around by paying as much as was possible and making special arrangements for his finances, but in the long run this was not enough to compensate for the hurt feelings between the two.

Unity of Command:

Authors only dealt with one superior, Perkins, but often more on paper than in person

Perkins did not violate the rule of unity of command in the sense of having his authors deal with more than one superior at Scribner's. In that area his behavior was in line with Fayol's ideal. All of his authors dealt directly with him, with the exception of Wheelock's copy editing of Wolfe's work. Even this does not really violate the principle in spirit, for it was merely a matter of getting staff help on an enormous project that Perkins was already devoting too much time to.

However, Fayol considered one of the important aspects of unity of command to be verbal orders, and "no abuse of written communication." Perkins would have disagreed. He was a voluminous letter writer. He sent long critiques to his authors of all their work, and his usual mode was to react to any manuscript quickly by wire, following up with a detailed letter.

One of the primary differences between Fayol's and Perkins' ways of communicating with employees is easily explained by the fact that Perkins was not dealing with present workers. His authors were scattered around the world, and long distance telephone service was not what it is now—and no e-mail! The telegram was his best way of communicating quickly to an author about sales, contract terms, and his opinion of the work. If this mode of communication is counted as verbal, since it was as close was he could get to direct verbal contact, then his actions are more in line with Fayol's principles. All of Perkins' written communication cannot be excused by distance, however, as he often wrote to authors in the same city.

But Fayol preferred verbal orders to written ones because "it is well known that differences and misunderstandings which a conversation could clear up, grow more bitter in writing." Ironically, this may be one of the reasons Perkins wrote such long letters. He went into great detail about his feelings on any subject, especially the author's work, to dispel any misunderstandings, often ending with, "If I could see you in person I know I could explain it better..."

All of Perkins' authors had great respect for the written word, which may have been another reason why Perkins used this form of communication so often. Given the reactions of his authors to his letters and suggestive critiques, it is hard to say that he "abused" it. He was true to the spirit of "unity of command," if not the letter of the principle.

Subordination of the Individual to the General Interest:

The highest priority was the work, which came first before personal gain, or personal or company profit.

Fayol's principle of the subordination of the individual to the general interest raises an interesting point regarding the management of creative people in particular. Fayol saw this principle as a tool for the manager to use in resolving conflicts: When the individual's own interest was contrary to that of the company, that of the company should prevail. Perkins, however, had a different set of priorities which, I conclude, is one of the main differences between managing creative people and managing others. This "Perkins Principle" will be discussed more fully below.

Applications to Specific Authors

F. Scott Fitzgerald

Remuneration of personnel came to take precedence over all else. Keeping Fitzgerald solvent kept him working on more important writing than his lucrative short stories, and was always mixed with equity as well as discipline. Unity of command became less important, as Fitzgerald did become friends with and communicate with Charles Scribner as well as Perkins. Perkins violated the principle of subordination to the general interest to keep Fitzgerald working on what was most important for his talents even when it appeared to not be in the best interest of Scribner's.

Ernest Hemingway

Although he required less attention than some authors, Hemingway's remuneration was important to him as well. This relationship worked out to be lucrative to both Hemingway and Scribner's almost from the start, and was more in line with Fayol's sub-principle of being fair to both employer and employee. However, Hemingway did not see money as the most important yardstick of the worth of his talent, and was more concerned about his own personal standards of excellence. Perkins' applications of equity and discipline were also important, as Hemingway needed to feel that he was being dealt with fairly all the time. In violation of Fayol's sub-principle encouraging verbal communication, Perkins communicated with Hemingway on paper often, although they would go off together for days on trips to talk about work and unrelated subjects. He knew that Hemingway's work was of paramount interest to him, and that took priority over company or personal interest.

Thomas Wolfe

Perkins' work with Wolfe is perhaps a good example of the manager's mistakes. Remuneration of personnel was important to Wolfe only in terms of what it said about his standing at Scribner's. Perkins' personal involvement became more important than the money which changed hands. Equity—especially in terms of devotion and loyalty—also came to bear here. Wolfe was devoted and loyal, and he demanded equal amounts in return, almost equal to his own extra-human proportions. Discipline was more difficult with someone like Wolfe. He followed Perkins' advice so closely in terms of the cuts that were suggested in his novels that he regretted it later when others dared to suggest that Perkins may have been wrong. The interest of the company meant little if anything to Wolfe, and Perkins once again used his work as the top priority for all involved. Although they spoke often in person, their correspondence is also lengthy. Perkins wrote to Wolfe when he knew what a violent reaction his suggestions and opinions would cause in his volatile writer. Wolfe, for his part, wrote to everyone including Perkins even when they were in the same city, extensively. But he also demanded the use of written communication during their break to formalize their relationship.

All told, it appears that Perkins was a good Fayol-style manager, albeit unknowingly, with notable exceptions which relate directly to the fact that he was working with creative people. His work was most in line with Fayol's ideas in the areas of equity, discipline, and remuneration of personnel, and at variance with Fayol in the areas of unity of command and subordination of the individual to the general interest. This would imply that managers of creative people would be wise to follow Fayol's guidelines, allowing for the "Perkins Principles," so to speak.

The "Perkins Principles"

A Matter of Priorities

The primary Perkins Principle has been mentioned above as a variation on Fayol's subordination to the general interest. The creative person is more likely to be motivated by subordinating all interests to the overriding one of improving the work rather than improving the bottom line of an organization.

One of the most common themes running through all of Perkins' work with his authors is contained in a phrase he wrote to Wolfe: "There is nothing so great as a book can be" (Perkins, 1950).

Despite Perkins' strong loyalty to his firm and to his authors, he had one higher loyalty that all his authors shared—to the work.

The work came first. Not just the current work, or most profitable work, or even the work in progress, but the overall work of a writer's career—Fitzgerald's post-flapper stories, Hemingway's longer, more substantive novels, all the books contained in Wolfe. Over and over again he said to them, "Just get back to work; we'll figure it out. Don't worry about the public, profits, Scribner's or even me. Don't even worry about yourself. Worry about the work." He told his superiors at Scribner's, "A publisher's first allegiance is to talent" (in Berg, 1978) and he impressed this priority on all of his authors.

This Perkins Principle can be important for the manager of creative people. Whereas Fayol would tell the manager that when an author's work was interfering with the company's interest, the company's interest should prevail, Perkins would say, "Let him work." This conflict between the two is very real and faced every day by managers.

By appealing to this side of the author, Perkins made them feel as though they were both working toward the same goal, making the work better. Because the writer worked almost exclusively with Perkins, he or she naturally felt, as Wolfe said many times, that all of Scribner's was there for the betterment of the writing. This may not have always been the Scribner's management's real goal, but the author felt that it was, or at least that it was for Perkins.

The results for Scribner's were mixed. A considerable amount of effort was put into Wolfe's works only to have him leave and go to another publishing house. This time may have been misspent in terms of benefits to the company.

However, in the long run, Scribner's for many years reaped the benefits of the classics which Perkins kept his authors working on. Most did not make money during the author's—or, in some cases, Perkins'—lifetime. But many publishing companies live off their own back lists, and eventually Scribner's made money from the major works of Perkins' three major authors. A detailed profit and loss analysis comparing the time and money spent versus the returns over the years is a bit beyond the limits of this work.

Perkins felt his first allegiance was to talent, and second, perhaps, to the long run good of the company. He left them quite a legacy.

The Power of Suggestion

Although Perkins varied from Fayol's dictum not to abuse written communication, the style of his letters could be one of his most important contributions to managerial guidelines.

There is a pattern that emerges in Perkins' letters. First, in a brief telegram, he praises whatever they have done in fulsome terms. Then in a follow up letter he goes on to discuss his "minor criticisms." He gives background and reasons for the negative as well as the positive comments, mentioning specifics in the manuscript. He also always makes it clear that his feelings are his alone, merely suggestions for the author to take and do with as he or she pleases. He then ends his letters with a phrase such as, "These are suggestions only, don't do anything about them now. We'll talk about them when you're here."

This ending has two effects. One, it cautions the author not to either race to the manuscript and start making changes right away, or, conversely, to begin brooding about why the editor thought so much was wrong. Invariably, it seems, the author would put the letter away, start thinking vaguely about the things Perkins had said, and eventually come around to most of the changes on his or her own.

Perkins' style of stating all of his orders in vague but suggestive terms allowed the creative person to do the creating. Even in the case of Wolfe, where many accused Perkins of actually writing his work, it is clear from the evidence that he made suggestions of large cuts, changes of emphasis and focus, rather than rewriting within sentences and actually creating.

From the reports of authors who worked with Perkins it is clear that his manner in person was similar—the silence, the vague phrase, the suggested idea dropped casually in conversation. All of these allowed the writer to do his or her own writing, but with their editors' guidance and perspective.

Room for Growth

There is one other area where Perkins' views differed from Fayol's theory, which illustrates another important part of his technique.

We have focused here on Fayol's "Process" principles. However, one of his "End result" principles is "stability of tenure of personnel." One classical critic, Haire (1962), interpreted Fayol's guidelines to mean a minimum of change within employees as well as within the system:

Very much growth and development in the individual will upset the system. He was put into a job that was an appropriate size for him. If he grows much bigger, he will either want to reach out and do more, which will upset the apple cart, or he will work only about half speed, which has deleterious effects upon his and other's morale.

Perkins' approach to his authors' growth was diametrically opposed to this. He constantly took on writers working on a project that was too small for the talents he saw in them, and then brought them along gradually to something more worthy of their gifts. This is true of Fitzgerald, whom he weaned away from flapper novels toward deeper works; Hemingway, whom he sustained through minor novels such as *To Have* and toward a major accomplishment such as *Bell*; and Wolfe, whom he pushed to finish one project so that he could hone his talent in future works that were burning to come out of him.

The evidence shows that Perkins' interpretation of stability of tenure would be to nurture the creative person along through stages of development to the kind of work that he or she will do best. This created stability in Perkins' situation, working for a publishing company that was "absolutely true to our authors and support(s) them loyally in the face of losses" (in Bruccoli, 1978; Fitzgerald and Perkins, 1971) through money losers to get them to write the greater work which would turn out to be lucrative as well.

Conclusion

My research was undertaken to explore the nature of the editor as manager, in the role of "muse" for writers and other creative people. To do this, I applied the guidelines developed by one successful manager, Henri Fayol, to the behavior of another, Maxwell Perkins.

The ultimate purpose is to give managers of creative people general guidelines to use. Despite the changes in the publishing industry in the intervening years, I hope that these conclusions can still be helpful to those tasked with managing creative people today.

Bibliography

Aswell, Edward C. (1941) "A Note on Thomas Wolfe," in Thomas Wolfe, *The Hills Beyond*. New York: Harper's.

Baker, Carlos. (1956) *Hemingway: The Writer as Artist*. Princeton, NJ: Princeton University Press.

Baker, Carlos. (1961) "Hemingway." *Saturday Review,* Vol. 44, July 29, p. 10-13.

Baker, Carlos. (1969) *Ernest Hemingway: A Life Story*. New York: Scribner's.

Barber, Phillip W. (1958) "Tom Wolfe Writes a Play," *Harper's Magazine,* Vol. 216, May, p. 73-74.

Berg, A. Scott. (1978) *Max Perkins: Editor of Genius*. New York: Dutton.

Brett, George P. (1913) "Book Publishing and Its Present Tendencies," *Atlantic,* Vol. 111, April, p. 454-55.

Brooks, Van Wyck. (1965) *Days of the Phoenix*. New York: Dutton.

Brown, John Mason. (1950) "Counselor-at-Large," *Still Seeing Things*. New York: McGraw-Hill.

Bruccoli, Matthew. (1963) *The Composition of "Tender Is the Night."* Pittsburgh: University of Pittsburgh Press.

Bruccoli, Matthew. (1972) "Introduction," *As Ever, Scott Fitzgerald—: Letters Between F. Scott Fitzgerald and His Literary Agent, Harold Ober, 1919-1940*. Philadelphia: Lippincott.

Bruccoli, Matthew. (1978) *Scott and Ernest: The Authority of Failure and the Authority of Success*. New York: Random House.

Burlingame, Roger. (1946) *Of Making Many Books*. New York: Scribner's.

Burt, Struthers. (1951) "Catalyst for Genius," *Saturday Review of Literature,* June 9, Vol. 34, p. 7.

Business Week. (1978) "Mastering Management in Creative Industries," May 29, p. 88.

Caldwell, Erskine. (1951) *Call It Experience*. New York: Duell.

Callaghan, Morley. (1963). *That Summer in Paris*. New York: Coward-McCann.

Canby, Henry Seidel. (1947) *American Memoir*. Boston: Houghton-Mifflin.

Canfield, Cass. (1975) "Review of *A History of Book Publishing in the United States* by J. Tebbel," *Publisher's Weekly,* Vol. 207, April 14, p. 23.

Chambers, P. (1974) "Europe's Greatest Management Pioneer." *International Management,* Vol. 29, June, p. 48-51.

Cousins, Norman. (1976) "The Hemingway Letters," *Saturday Review,* Vol. 4, October 2, p. 4-6

Cowley, Malcolm. (1944) "Unshaken Friend," *The New Yorker,* Vol. 20, Part I, April 1, p. 36, and Part II, April 8, p. 30.

Cowley, Malcolm. (1950) "On Writing as a Profession," *New Republic,* Vol. 122, April 24, p. 15.

Cowley, Malcolm. (1954) *The Literary Situation*. New York: Viking Press.

Cowley, Malcolm. (1956) *Exile's Return*. New York: Viking Press.

Cowley, Malcolm. (1957) "Miserly Millionaire of Words." *Reporter,* Vol. 16, February 7, p. 38-40.

Cunliffe, Marcus. (1964) *The Literature of the U. S.* London, Baltimore: Penguin Books.

DeVoto, Bernard. (1936) "Genius Is Not Enough," *Saturday Review of Literature,* April 25.

Donaldson, Norman and Donaldson, Betty. (1980) *How Did They Die?* New York: St. Martin's Press.

Donaldson, Scott. (1977) *By Force of Will: The Life and Art of Ernest Hemingway* New York: Viking Press.

Dyer, Frederic and Dyer, John (1969). *Bureaucracy vs. Creativity.* Coral Gables, FL: University of Miami Press.

Eble, Kenneth. (1964) "Craft of Revision: *The Great Gatsby.*" *American Literature,* Vol. 36, November, p. 315-26.

Epstein, Joseph. (1978) "Grey Eminence with a Blue Pencil," *Times Literary Supplement,* July 28.

Fayol, Henri. (1949) *General and Industrial Management,* London: Pitman, Translated from the French edition by Constance Storrs.

Fitzgerald, F. Scott. (1951) "Financing Finnegan." In *The Stories of F. Scott Fitzgerald,* ed Malcolm Cowley, New York: Scribner's, p. 449-50.

Fitzgerald, F. Scott. (1963a) *Letters,* ed. by Andrew Turnbull. New York: Scribner's.

Fitzgerald, F. Scott. (1963b) "Love to All of You, Of All Generations," *Esquire,* Vol. 60, #1, July, p. 90.

Fitzgerald, F. Scott. (1980) *The Correspondence of F. Scott Fitzgerald,* ed. by Matthew Bruccoli. New York: Random House.

Fitzgerald, F. Scott and Ober, Harold. (1972) *As Ever, Scott Fitzgerald—: Letters Between F. Scott Fitzgerald and His Literary Agent, Harold Ober, 1919-1940*, ed. by Matthew Bruccoli. Philadelphia: Lippincott.

Fitzgerald, F. Scott and Perkins, Maxwell E. (1971) *Dear Scott/Dear Max: The Fitzgerald-Perkins Correspondence.* New York: Scribner's.

Gibson, James L., John M. Iyancevich, and James H. Donnelly, Jr. (1976) *Organizational Behavior, Structure, Processes.* Dallas, TX: Business Publications, Inc..

Gingrich, Arnold. (1966) "Scott, Ernest and Whoever," *Esquire*, Vol. 66, December, p. 187.

Graham, Sheilah. (1976) *The Real F. Scott Fitzgerald: 35 Years Later.* New York: Grosset and Dunlop.

Graham, Sheilah, and Gerold Frank. (1958) *Beloved Infidel: The Education of a Woman.* New York: Holt.

Haire, Mason. (1962) "The Concept of Power and the Concept of Man," in *Social Science Approaches to Business Behavior*, ed. by George B. Strother. Homewood, IL: The Dorsey Press.

Halberstadt, John. (1981) "Who Wrote Tom Wolfe's Last Novels?" *New York Review of Books,* Vol. 28, March 19, p. 51-52.

Hale, Nancy. (1968) "Can Writers Ignore Critics?" *Saturday Review*, Vol. 51, March 23, p. 24.

Hatcher, Harlan. (1935) *Creating the Modern American Novel.* New York: Farrar, Straus and Rinehart.

Hemingway, Gregory. (1976) *Papa.* Boston: Houghton-Mifflin.

Hemingway, Leicester. (1962) *My Brother, Ernest Hemingway.* Cleveland: World.

Hoffman, Frederick J. (1951) *The Modern Novel in America.* Chicago: Regenery.

Holman, C. Hugh. (1960) "Thomas Wolfe," *Pamphlets on American Writers.* Minnesota: University of Minnesota.

Hoffman, Frederick J. (1955) *The Twenties: American Writing in the Postwar Decade.* New York: Viking Press.

Holman, C. Hugh. (1978) "What an Editor Is," *Sewanee Review,* Vol. 86, Fall, p. 575.

James, T. F. (1957) "Hemingway at Work." *Cosmopolitan,* Vol. 143, August, p. 52-55.

Kazin, Alfred. (1955) "Writer's Friend," in *Inmost Leaf: A Selection of Essays.* New York: Harcourt, Brace.

Knopf, Alfred A. (1950) "The Man Who Made Great Novels Greater," *New York Times Book Review,* March 26, p. 3.

Kuehl, John and Bryer, Jackson R. (1971) "Introduction," in *Dear Scott/Dear Max: The Fitzgerald-Perkins Correspondence.* New York: Scribner's.

Lardner, Ring and Maxwell Perkins. (1973) *Ring Around Max: The Correspondence of Ring Lardner and Max Perkins.* Ed. Clifford M. Carruthers. DeKalb, IL: Northern Illinois University Press.

Little, Thomas. (1947) "The Thomas Wolfe Collection of William B. Wisdom," *Harvard Library Bulletin,* Vol. 1, p.283.

Lynn, Kenneth S. (1978) "Strange Unhappy Life of Max Perkins," *Commentary,* Vol. 66, December, p. 59.

Madison, Charles. (1966) "Writers and Publishers," *The American Scholar,* Vol. 35, Summer, p. 531, 533.

McCormick, Ken. (1962) "Editors Today," in *Editors on Editing*, ed. Gerald Gross. New York: Grosset and Dunlop, p. 27.

Middlebrook, L. Ruth. (1947) "Further Memories of Tom Wolfe," *American Mercury*, Vol. 64, April, p. 418.

Mizener, Arthur. (1974) *The Far Side of Paradise*. New York: Avon.

Mooney, J. D. (1947) *The Principles of Organization*. New York: Harper Brothers Publishers.

Muller, Herbert J. (1947) *Thomas Wolfe*, Norfolk, CT: New Directions Books.

Nation. (1940) "White Collar Salaries," Vol. 150, May 25, p. 642.

New York Times. (1947), "M. E. Perkins, 62, Scribner's Editor," June 18, p. 25.

Newsweek. (1958) "Hemingway: He Writes in an Icy Mood.," Vol. 51, April 21, p. 122-23.

Nowell, Elizabeth. (1956) "Introduction," *The Letters of Thomas Wolfe*. New York: Scribner's.

Nowell, Elizabeth. (1960) *Thomas Wolfe: A Biography*. Garden City, NY: Doubleday.

Parsons, Geoffrey. (1950) "The Man Who Guided and Edited Fitzgerald, Hemingway and Wolfe," *New York Herald Tribune Books*, March 26, p. 5.

Pearson, Norman N. (1945) "Fayolism as the Necessary Complement of Taylorism." *American Politicial Science Review*, Vol. 39, February.

Perkins, Maxwell. (1950) *Editor to Author: The Letters of Maxwell E. Perkins*. New York: Charles Scribner's Sons.

Plimpton, George. (1974) "An Interview with Ernest Hemingway." In *Ernest Hemingway: Five Decades of Criticism*, Ed. Linda W. Wagner, Michigan: Michigan State University Press, p. 21-38.

Prigozy, Ruth. (1971) "Matter of Measure: The Tangled Relationship Between Fitzgerald and Hemingway," *Commonweal*, Vol. 95, October. 29, p. 104.

Pritchett, V. S. (1973) "Gentleman's Agreement," *New Statesman*, March 23, p. 417.

Publisher's Weekly. (1932) "Charles Scribner Elected President of Scribner's," Vol. 122, October 1, p. 1339.

Rawlings, Marjorie Kinnan. (1950) "Portrait of a Magnificent Editor as Seen in His Letters," *Publisher's Weekly*, Vol. 157, April 1, p. 1573.

Reeves, George, Jr. (1958) "A Note on the Life and Letters of Thomas Wolfe," *South Atlantic Quarterly*, Vol. 57, p.219-20.

Reeves, Paschal. (1965) "Thomas Wolfe on Publishers: Reaction to Rejection," *South Atlantic Quarterly*, Vol. 64, Summer, p.387.

Ross, Lillian. (1962) "How Do You Like It Now, Gentlemen?" in *Hemingway: A Collection of Critical Essays*, ed. by Robert Perry Weeks. New York: Prentice-Hall.

Sadleir, Michael. (1950) "Books and Writers," *Spectator*, Vol. 185, August 25, p. 246.

Scribner, Charles, Jr. "Confessions of a Book Publisher: Scribner's Address, April 12, 1977," *Publisher's Weekly*, Vol. 211, June 6, 1977, p.47

Skipp, Francis Edwin.(1962). "Thomas Wolfe and His Scribner's Editors." Dissertation. Durham, NC: Duke University.

Skipp, Francis Edwin.(1967-8). "Thomas Wolfe Maxwell Perkins and Politics," *Modern Fiction Studies,* Vol. 13, Winter.

Sloane, William M. (1938) "Literary prospecting," *Saturday Review of Literature,* Vol. 19, December 3, p. 3-4.

Smith, Chard Powers. (1962) "Perkins and the Elect," *The Antioch Review,* Spring, Vol. 22, p. 85-6.

Smith, Harrison. (1947) "Midwife to Literature: Maxwell Evarts Perkins," *Saturday Review of Literature,* Vol. 30, July 12, p. 16.

Smith, Harrison. (1949) "Writer vs. the Publisher," *Saturday Review of Literature,* Vol. 32, December 17, p. 20.

Smith, R. H. (1969) "Authors and Editors." *Publisher's Weekly,* Vol. 195, March 31, p. 15-17.

Stein, Gertrude. "Ernest Hemingway and the Postwar Decade." *Atlantic Monthly,* Vol. 152, August, p. 197-208.

Stern, Edith M. (1942) "Charles Scribner's Sons," *Saturday Review of Literature,* Vol. 25, January 17, p. 14-15.

Stevens, Virginia. (1958) "Tom Wolfe's America," *Mainstream,* January, Vol. 11. p. 20

Tassin, Algernon. (1914a) "American Authors and Their Publishers: Part I—When Bryant Comes to Town," *The Bookman,* Vol. 39, April, p. 178-88.

Tassin, Algernon. (1914b) "American Authors and Their Publishers: Part II—When the Pen Began to Pay," *The Bookman,* Vol. 39, May, p. 275.

Tassin, Algernon. (1914c) "American Authors and Their Publishers: Part III—When War Was in the Air," *The Bookman,* Vol. 39, June, p. 378-88.

Terry, John Skally. (1953) "Wolfe and Perkins," *Enigma of Thomas Wolfe,* ed. by Richard Weber. Cambridge: Harvard University of Press.

Turnbull, Andrew. (1962) *Scott Fitzgerald.* New York: Scribner's.

Urwick, Lyndall F. (1969) "The Functions of Administration, with Special Reference to the Work of Henri Fayol," in Luther Gulick and Lyndall Urwick, eds., *Papers in the Science of Administration,* New York: Augustus M. Kelley.

Volkening, Henry T. (1939) "Thomas Wolfe: Penance No More." *Virginia Quarterly Review,* Spring, Vol. 15, p. 196-215.

Weeks, Edward. (1950) "Peripatetic Reviewer," *Atlantic Monthly,* Vol. 185, April, p. 79.

Wheelock, John Hall. (1950) "Introduction," in Maxwell E. Perkins, *Editor to Author: The Letters of Maxwell E. Perkins.* New York: Charles Scribner's Sons, p. 203.

Wolfe, Thomas. (1940) *You Can't Go Home Again.* New York: Harper's.

Wolfe, Thomas. (1943) *Tom Wolfe's Letters to His Mother, Julia Elizabeth Wolfe.* New York: Scribner's.

Wolfe, Thomas. (1946) "Writing Is My Life: The Letters of Thomas Wolfe," *Atlantic Monthly,* Vol. 178, December, p. 60.

Wolfe, Thomas. (1956) *The Letters of Thomas Wolfe.* New York: Scribner's.

Wren, Daniel. (1972) *Evolution of Management Thought.* New York: Ronald Press Co.

About the Author

Kathleen Dixon Donnelly, PhD

Kathleen Dixon Donnelly, has been involved in teaching and the creative process for over 40 years. Her dissertation for her Ph.D. in Communications from Dublin City University, "Such Friends," was on the creative development of writers in early 20th century salons. *Manager as Muse* is based on her thesis for her MBA from Duquesne University in her hometown of Pittsburgh, Pennsylvania.

Currently Kathleen is senior lecturer at Birmingham City University. She has published a series of books from her blogs as Gypsy Teacher at www.lulu.com/gypsyteacher, chronicling her voyages on Semester at Sea and relocation to the United Kingdom. She also posts about early 20th century writers at www.suchfriends.wordpress.com with updates on Twitter, @SuchFriends.

Kathleen lives with her Irish Husband Tony Dixon and their two cats, William Butler Yeats and Lady Augusta Gregory, in Birmingham, UK.

You can contact her at kaydee@ gypsyteacher.com.

www.ingramcontent.com/pod-product-compliance
Lightning Source LLC
Chambersburg PA
CBHW051641170526
45167CB00001B/276